新双双中文教材 12

New Chinese Language and Culture Course

中国文学欣赏 Appreciation of Chinese Literature

（第二版）

[美]王双双　编著

北京大学出版社
PEKING UNIVERSITY PRESS

图书在版编目（CIP）数据

中国文学欣赏/（美）王双双编著. —2版. —北京：北京大学出版社，2022.8
新双双中文教材
ISBN 978-7-301-33068-5

Ⅰ.①中…　Ⅱ.①王…　Ⅲ.①文学欣赏—中国—对外汉语教学—教材　Ⅳ.①H195.4

中国版本图书馆CIP数据核字（2022）第142550号

书　　　名	中国文学欣赏（第二版） ZHONGGUO WENXUE XINSHANG（DI-ER BAN）
著作责任者	［美］王双双　编著
英文翻译	张瓅月
责任编辑	邓晓霞
标准书号	ISBN 978-7-301-33068-5
出版发行	北京大学出版社
地　　　址	北京市海淀区成府路205号　100871
网　　　址	http://www.pup.cn　　新浪微博：@北京大学出版社
电子信箱	zpup@pup.cn
电　　　话	邮购部 010-62752015　发行部 010-62750672　编辑部 010-62753334
印　刷　者	北京宏伟双华印刷有限公司
经　销　者	新华书店 889毫米×1194毫米　16开本　11.75印张　236千字 2007年5月第1版 2022年8月第2版　2022年8月第1次印刷
定　　　价	88.00元（含课本、练习本、音频）

未经许可，不得以任何方式复制或抄袭本书之部分或全部内容。
版权所有，侵权必究
举报电话：010-62752024　电子信箱：fd@pup.pku.edu.cn
图书如有印装质量问题，请与出版部联系，电话：010-62756370

第二版序

能够与北京大学出版社合作出版"双双中文教材"的第二版，让这套优秀的对外汉语教材泽被更多的学生，加州中文教学研究中心倍感荣幸。

这是一套洋溢着浓浓爱意的教材。作者的女儿在美国出生，到了识字年龄，作者教她学习过市面上流行的多套中文教材，但都强烈地感觉到这些教材"水土不服"。一解女儿学习中文的燃眉之急，是作者编写这套教材的初衷和原动力。为了让没有中文环境的孩子能够喜欢学习中文，作者字斟句酌地编写课文；为了赋予孩子审美享受、引起他们的共鸣，作者特邀善画儿童创作了一幅幅稚气可爱的插图；为了加深孩子们对内容的理解，激发孩子们的学习热情，作者精心设计了充满创造性的互动活动。

这是一套承载着文化传承使命感的教材。语言不仅仅是文化的载体，更是文化重要的有机组成部分。学习一门外语的深层障碍往往根植于目标语言与母语间的文化差异。这种差异对于学习中文的西方学生尤为突出。这套教材的使用对象正处在好奇心和好胜心最强的年龄阶段，作者抓住了这一特点，变阻力为动力，一改过去削学生认知能力和智力水平之"足"以适词汇和语言知识之"履"的通病。教材在高年级部分，一个学期一个文化主题，以对博大精深的中国文化的探索激发学生的学习兴趣，使学生在学习语言的同时了解璀璨的中国文化。

"双双中文教材"自2005年面世以来，受到了老师、学生和家长的广泛欢迎。很多觉得中文学习枯燥无味而放弃的学生，因这套教材发现了学习中文的乐趣，又重新回到了中文课堂。本次修订，作者不仅吸纳了老师们对于初版的反馈意见和自己实际使用过程中的心得，还参考了近年对外汉语教学理论及实践方面的成果。语言学习部分由原来的九册改为五册，一学年学习一册，文化学习部分保持一个专题一册。相信修订后的"新双双中文教材"会更方便、实用，让更多学生受益。

张晓江
美国加州中文教学研究中心秘书长

第一版前言

"双双中文教材"是一套专门为海外青少年编写的中文课本,是我在美国八年的中文教学实践基础上编写成的。在介绍这套教材之前,请读一首小诗:

> 一双神奇的手,
> 推开一扇窗。
> 一条神奇的路,
> 通向灿烂的中华文化。

鲍凯文　鲍维江

鲍维江和鲍凯文姐弟俩是美国生美国长的孩子,也是我的学生。1998年冬,他们送给我的新年贺卡上的小诗,深深地打动了我的心。我把这首诗看成我文化教学的"回声"。我要传达给海外每位中文老师:我教给他们(学生)中国文化,他们思考了、接受了、回应了。这条路走通了!

语言是一种交流的工具,更是一种文化和一种生活方式,所以学习中文也就离不开中华文化的学习。汉字是一种古老的象形文字,她从远古走来,带有大量的文化信息,但学起来并不容易。使学生增强兴趣、减小难度,走出苦学汉字的怪圈,走进领悟中华文化的花园,是我编写这套教材的初衷。

学生不论大小,天生都有求知的欲望,都有欣赏文化美的追求。中华文化本身是魅力十足的。把这宏大而玄妙的文化,深入浅出地,有声有色地介绍出来,让这迷人的文化如涓涓细流,一点一滴地渗入学生们的心田,使学生们逐步体味中国文化,是我编写这套教材的目的。

为此我将汉字的学习放入文化介绍的流程之中同步进行,让同学们在学中国地理的同时,学习汉字;在学中国历史的同时,学习汉字;在学中国哲学的同时,学习汉字;在学中国科普文选的同时,学习汉字……

这样的一种中文学习,知识性强,趣味性强;老师易教,学生易学。当学生们合上书本时,他们的眼前是中国的大好河山,是中国五千年的历史和妙不可言的哲学思维,是奔腾的现代中国……

总之,他们了解了中华文化,就会探索这片土地,热爱这片土地,就会与中国结下情缘。

最后我要衷心地感谢所有热情支持和帮助我编写教材的老师、家长、学生、朋友和家人。特别是老同学唐玲教授、何茜老师和我女儿Uta Guo年复一年的鼎力相助。可以说这套教材是大家努力的结果。

王双双

课程设置（建议）

序号	书名	适用年级
1	中文课本　第一册	幼儿园/一年级
2	中文课本　第二册	二年级
3	中文课本　第三册	三年级
4	中文课本　第四册	四年级
5	中文课本　第五册	五年级
6	中国成语故事	六年级
7	中国地理常识	六年级
8	中国古代故事	七年级
9	中国神话传说	七年级
10	中国古代科学技术	八年级
11	中国民俗与民间艺术	八年级
12	中国文学欣赏	九年级
13	中国诗歌欣赏	九年级
14	中国古代哲学	十年级
15	中国历史	十年级

目录

第一课　　武松打虎 …………………………… 1

第二课　　女儿国 ……………………………… 11

第三课　　草船借箭（上）…………………… 21

第四课　　草船借箭（下）…………………… 30

第五课　　孙悟空三打白骨精 ………………… 40

第六课　　陋室铭 ……………………………… 51

第七课　　鸡毛信 ……………………………… 58

第八课　　考试 ………………………………… 70

第九课　　《卧虎藏龙》选段 ………………… 80

第十课　　宝玉和黛玉 ………………………… 90

生字表（简）…………………………………… 101

生字表（繁）…………………………………… 103

生词表（简）…………………………………… 105

生词表（繁）…………………………………… 107

第一课

武松打虎

武松是一位梁山好汉。一次在回家的路上，要经过一座山。来到山前，武松看见一个酒店。他走得又累又渴，就进去买酒喝。他一口气喝了三大碗，喝完了还要店家给他添酒，店家却不肯添。武松问："为什么不给我添酒？"店家说："这种酒叫'三碗不过冈'，是说人喝了三碗之后就会醉倒。"武松听了哈哈大笑说："我喝酒是海量，从来没醉过。"店家又说："前面的山叫景阳冈，最近出了一只老虎，已经吃了好几个人。你酒喝多了，可不能上山了。"武松不信，只管要酒。结果武松一共喝了十八碗。喝完酒，武松不听店家的劝告，提着一根棍子上山去了。

刘继卣（yōu）　绘

来到山脚下，他看见一张官府的布告，才知道真的有虎。他想："我有棍子，怕什么虎！"就继续往前走。这时，太阳已经落山了。武松觉得身上热起来，头也有些晕了，原来他的酒喝得太多了。他看见路边有一块大石头，就把棍子放在一边，往石头上一躺，睡着了。

忽然，刮起一阵大风，把武松惊醒了，一只凶猛的大老虎从树林里扑了出来。武松"啊呀"一声，从大石头上翻身跳起，酒也吓醒了。只见老虎瞪着两只眼睛向他扑来。武松一闪，老虎扑了个空，气得大吼一声，声音像打雷一样。老虎又把尾巴竖起来，向武松一扫，武松再一闪，又躲开了。趁着老虎还没转过身来，武松连忙抓起棍子，用尽全身的力气向老虎打去。没想到武松打得太急，打到了树上，棍子断成了两截。这时，老虎又向武松扑过来，武松往后一跳，老虎正好扑到他眼前。武松扔下棍子，用双手死死抓住老虎的头，用尽所有的力气往下按。老虎被紧紧地按在地上，两只爪子在地上乱抓。老虎渐渐没有气力了。

刘继卣　绘

第一课

武松又抬起脚往老虎的头上乱踢，举起铁锤般的拳头，照着老虎的头使劲地打，打了几十下，老虎就一点儿也不动了。

武松独自一人赤手空拳打死老虎的事情很快就传开了。大家都争先恐后地来看打虎的英雄。官府给了武松一些赏钱，他把这些钱都分给了辛苦打虎的猎人们。从此他更受大家的敬重了。

（根据施耐庵著《水浒传》选段改编）

作品简介

《水浒传》是中国第一部以白话文写出的长篇小说，作者施耐庵是元末明初人。《水浒传》《三国演义》《西游记》《红楼梦》被称为"中国古典四大名著"。

《水浒传》讲的是梁山一百零八个好汉的故事。书中人物个性鲜明，活跃生动。他们都爱打抱不平，反对贪官，被迫上梁山，起义造反。他们重朋友、轻生死、讲义气的行为，体现了当时中国大众的道德观念。

《水浒传》故事曲折、语言生动，被翻译成多种文字。其中英文版的书名也被译为 *All Men Are Brothers*。

- 听歌曲《好汉歌》
- 看视频《武松醉打蒋门神》

生词

liáng shān 梁山	Mount Liang	chèn zhe 趁着	take advantage of
jiǔ diàn 酒店	hotel, inn	yòng jìn 用尽	run out of
gāng 冈	ridge	liǎng jié 两截	two parts
quàn gào 劝告	advice	zhèng hǎo 正好	just in time
bù gào 布告	bulletin, notice	tiě chuí 铁锤	hammer
jì xù 继续	continue	shǐ jìn 使劲	exert all one's strength
yūn 晕	dizzy	chì shǒu kōng quán 赤手空拳	bare-handed
pū 扑	pounce	zhēng xiān kǒng hòu 争先恐后	strive to be the first and fear to lag behind
hǒu 吼	roar		
shù 竖	erect, stand	shǎng qian 赏钱	money reward

听写

酒店　劝告　布告　继续　晕　扑　吼　竖　趁着

正好　使劲　赤手空拳　争先恐后　*冈　赏钱

比一比

趁 { 趁早 / 趁着 }　　赏 { 赏钱 / 欣赏 }　　{ 锤（铁锤）/ 睡（睡觉）}

栽　　　截

栽树　　两截

组词游戏

店

酒店——饭店——旅店——书店——商店——小吃店——文具店

百货商店——冷饮店——理发店——洗衣店——美容店

近义词

好汉——英雄　　　　使劲——尽力——用力

反义词

竖——横　　　　不肯——同意

继续——停止

多音字

chuán	zhuàn
传	传
传开	水浒传

词语运用

趁着

① 趁着天还没黑，你赶快回家吧。

② 趁着饭还热，赶快吃吧。

③ 趁着爸爸有假，咱们全家去黄石公园旅游吧。

争先恐后

① 人们争先恐后地买票观看世界杯足球赛。

② 天气太热，人们争先恐后地去海边游泳。

③ 同学们争先恐后地报名参加暑期夏令营。

词语解释

海量——很大的酒量。

惊醒——受惊动而从睡眠中醒来。

敬重——恭敬尊重。

写作练习

如何写出生动的句子

{ 武松听了大笑。
{ 武松听了哈哈大笑。（写了笑声）

{ 只见老虎向武松扑来。
{ 只见老虎瞪着两只眼睛向武松扑来。（写了老虎的眼神）

{ 老虎扑了两下没扑着,气得大吼一声。
{ 老虎扑了两下没扑着,气得大吼一声,声音好像打雷一样。

（把老虎的吼声比喻成雷声）

阅读

(快板)

武松打虎

孙婧文　画

梁山英雄武二郎，
回家路过景阳冈。
口发干来肚子饿，
一家酒店在路旁。

酒店写着五个字：
"三碗不过冈！"
武松上前问仔细，
说是有虎在冈上。
吃人伤人已不少，
酒过三碗过不了冈。

武松听完哈哈笑，
咱天生就是有胆量。
武松喝酒十八碗，
提棍走上景阳冈。
身发热来头发晕，
一块石头上面躺。

忽然大风四方起。
跳出老虎口大张。
吼声如雷扑过来，
武松跳起闪一旁。

武松双手举起棍，
照着虎头就是一棒(bàng)。
只听"咔嚓(kā chā)"一声响，
棍子打在大树上。
断成两截不能用，
赤手空拳打一场。

武松手抓老虎头，
紧紧按在土地上。
拳打脚踢猛虎死，
再也不能把人伤！
这就是，武松打虎景阳冈，
英雄美名天下扬。

Lesson One

Wu Song Fights the Tiger

One day, Wu Song, one of the heroes in Liangshan Marsh, came to a mountain on his way home. At the foot of the mountain which he had to climb over, he saw an inn. Tired and thirsty, he went in and ordered wine to drink. After finishing three large bowls in one single gulp, he asked the owner for more but was refused. "Why don't you sell me more?" asked Wu Song. The owner replied, "This wine is called No Passing the Hill after Three Bowls, meaning anyone drinking after three bowls will get drunk." Hearing this, Wu Song laughed out loud, saying, "I have a hollow leg and never get drunk." The owner said again, "The mountain in the front is called Jingyang Hill. Lately a tiger appears inside. It has eaten several people. You have drunk too much wine. Don't walk inside the mountain." Wu Song didn't believe him and insisted on getting more wine. In the end he drank eighteen bowls of wine in total. After finishing drinking, not heeding the owner's advice, Wu Song walked to the mountain with his stick in hand.

At the foot of the mountain, upon seeing an official notice, Wu Song realized that indeed there was a tiger. He thought, "I have my staff. Why should I fear a tiger?" so he walked on. At that time, the sun had set and Wu Song felt a little hot and light-headed for he indeed drank too much wine. Seeing a big rock on the roadside, he put his stick aside, lay on the rock and fell asleep.

All of a sudden, Wu Song was wakened up with a start by a gust of wind to see a fierce tiger pouncing out from the woods towards him. With an "ah" coming out from his mouth, Wu Song turned his body and jumped up from the boulder, completely awake by fear from the hangover. With two eyes glaring, the tiger charged at him. Wu Song dodged his body; the tiger missed him. It was so agitated and roared like a thunder. It cocked its tail and swept Wu Song, who dodged again and escaped. Grasping the chance that the tiger had not yet turned around, Wu Song quickly grabbed the stick and hit the tiger with all his might. Unexpectedly, because Wu Song hit in such a hurry that the stick hit the tree and broke into two pieces. In the meanwhile, the tiger pounced again towards Wu Song. Wu Song leapt back, and the tiger fell down right before him. Wu Song threw away his staff and used his two hands to hold the tiger's head with all his might and pushed it down. Pressed tightly to the ground, its paws scratching at the ground, the tiger gradually ran out of breath. Wu Song lifted his feet and kicked the tiger's head, raised his hammer-like fists and hit the tiger's head hard. He hit it a few dozen times and finally the tiger ceased any movement.

The story of Wu Song killing the tiger all by himself with bare hand spread in no time. Everyone came eagerly to see the hero who beat the tiger. The local government gave Wu Song some reward

money, but he distributed the money among the hunters who previously worked hard to hunt the tiger. Because of this he was even more respected by all people.

(Adapted from excerpts from Water Margin by Shi Nai'an)

Brief Introduction of the Work

The *Water Margin* is the first novel written in vernacular Chinese by Shi Nai'an, a native of the late Yuan and early Ming dynasties. *Water Margin, Romance of the Three Kingdoms, Journey to the West*, and *Dream of the Red Chamber* are known as the "Four Great Classical Novels of China".

The *Water Margin* tells the story of one hundred and eight heroes abiding in the Mount Liang. The characters in the book are active and vivid with distinct personalities. They all loved to fight against the corrupt officials, and were all forced to Mount Liang to rebel against the hierarchy. They valued friendship and righteousness over life and didn't fear death, reflecting the moral values of the Chinese public at that time.

The story of The *Water Margin* with its twists and turns and vivid language has been translated into many languages. The English version of the book is also titled *All Men Are Brothers*.

- Listen to the *Song of Heroes* of the TV series *Water Margin*"
- Watch the video "*Wu Song Drunkenly Beats Jiang Menshen(door god)*"

第二课

女儿国

唐朝有个书生叫唐敖(áo)，他和朋友林之洋、多九公一起到国外去经商。

他们在大海上航行了很久。一天，他们看到了一片陆地，上岸以后，发现这里无论种地的、做工的还是做买卖的都是女人。她们说话都粗声大气的，还穿着男人的衣服。唐敖他们觉得非常奇怪。三人来到一家客店，一个穿着男人衣服的女人出来欢迎他们，说自己是客店老板。她回头招呼手下人来帮忙，出来的是一个穿着女人衣服的男人。他虽然身材高大，脸上还长着胡子，可是走起路来扭扭捏捏的，说话也细声细气的，脸上还擦着香粉和胭脂呢！唐敖他们觉得这真是稀奇古怪，别扭极了。

刘艺　画

渐渐地，唐敖他们才明白，这个地方叫女儿国，女人是管理国家大事的，在外做事的都是女人，男人反而在家里做家务。唐敖他们在街上做了几天买卖，有人来对他们说："你们的首饰和化妆品非常好，我们的国王想买些给宫女们用，你们进宫去谈谈价钱吧。"

不料进宫后，女国王一见到他们，就看上了林之洋，不由分说就封了林之洋做"娘娘"。马上一大群宫女就来给林之洋换衣服、戴花儿、擦胭脂；有人见他没有耳朵眼儿，拿起针就给他扎了两个，疼得他直叫；还有人看到他没有缠足，就拿来布条，把他的两只脚紧紧地缠了起来。林之洋疼得不能走路，觉得缠足太痛苦了，就自己剪断布条把脚放开了。国王知道了，非常生气地说："你这样不守规矩，怎么行呢？"于是叫人把林之洋狠狠地打了一顿，关了起来，准备过几天再与他结婚。

唐敖和多九公回到客店，左思右想，想出了一个办法：结婚以前，新娘是不能在丈夫家住的。于是他们对国王说："林之洋必须回客店住，等结婚的时候，您再派人来接他进宫吧。"国王答应了，但派了许多人看守客店。

晚上，趁着夜色，唐敖和多九公背着浑身是伤的林之洋，躲过卫兵，急急忙忙跑出客店，上船逃离了这个古怪的女儿国。

（根据李汝(rǔ)珍著《镜花缘(yuán)》选段改编）

生词

jīng shāng 经商	engage in trade	shǒu shi 首饰	jewelry
zhāo hu 招呼	call	huà zhuāng pǐn 化妆品	cosmetics
shēn cái 身材	stature, figure	tán 谈	talk
niǔ nie 扭捏	affectedly bashful	bù yóu fēn shuō 不由分说	allowing no explanation
cā 擦	wipe	dài 戴	wear
yān zhi 胭脂	rouge	zhā 扎	prick
xī qí gǔ guài 稀奇古怪	peculiar, bizarre	chán 缠	wrap, bind
biè niu 别扭	inharmonious, awkward	hún shēn 浑身	all over

听写

经商　招呼　身材　擦　胭脂　别扭　首饰　化妆品

谈　戴　浑身　*稀奇古怪　缠

比一比

经 { 经商 / 经常 / 经过

招 { 招呼 / 招待 / 招手

化 { 化妆 / 化学

首 { 首饰 / 首都

炎	谈	淡
炎热	谈话	淡水

组词游戏

谈

谈话——谈天——谈心——谈价钱——谈买卖

谈天说地——谈一谈——谈恋爱——谈情说爱

反义词

扭扭捏捏——大大方方　　稀奇古怪——普普通通

粗声大气——细声细气　　高大——矮小

多音字

biè	bié
别	别
别扭	别人

词语运用

反而

① 女儿国里女人在外做事，男人反而在家里做家务。

② "画蛇添足"意思是做了多余的事反而不好。

③ 医生说天天吃大鱼大肉，对身体反而不好。

招呼

① 他一见到老师，就笑着打招呼。

② 不论见到同学还是老师我都会马上打招呼。

③ 班长招呼同学都来帮忙搬东西。

词语解释

做买卖——经商，做生意。

家务——家事，指日常生活扫地、做饭等。

思考题

● 如果你是男生，读了《女儿国》会有什么想法？

● 如果你是女生，又会有什么样的想法？

阅读

君子国

[清] 李汝珍

"君子国"是个好让不争的礼乐之邦(bāng)。国主要求臣民不能给官员送东西，如果送东西就要治罪。这里的宰相平易近人，可亲可敬。这里的人民举止言谈十分有礼，路上行人相互让

路；卖主卖好货要钱不多，顾客主动付(fù)高价，彼(bǐ)此相让不下。作者用想象中的"君子国"表现他的理想生活，和对社会生活中的欺(qī)压、欺骗行为的不满。

资料

作品简介

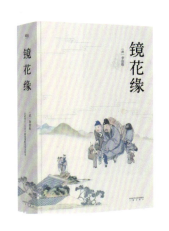

《镜花缘》是清代小说家李汝珍（约1763—约1830）写的一部思想开放、想象新奇的小说。故事讲述了武则天当皇帝时，书生唐敖和朋友林之洋、多九公出海经商的神奇见闻。"女儿国"就是其中的一个故事。在"女儿国"里，男子管理家务，女子管理国家大事。从皇帝到大臣都是女子。作者以幽默的方式对男尊女卑(bēi)提出疑问。

中国的女皇帝——武则天

中国历史上有没有女皇帝？回答是："有。"她叫武则天（624—705）。武则天原是唐朝的一位皇后，后来当了皇帝，改国号为"周"。她发明了一个汉字"曌(zhào)"作为自己的名字，意思是日月当空，光照大地。她管理国家几十年，社会安定，人口增加，农业、手工业和商业都有发展。武则天当皇帝时，也有女官，她用人不看门第只看能力，可以说她是中国古代一位了不起的女政治家。

武则天

Lesson Two

The Kingdom of Women

In Tang Dynasty, a scholar named Tang Ao went overseas with his friends Lin Zhiyang and Duojiu Gong to do business.

One day after they sailed in the sea for a long time, they saw a piece of land. They got ashore and found out that in this land it's all women who farmed the land, did the manual work, and ran business. These women spoke in loud voices and wore men's clothing, which in their eyes was very bizarre. When the three of them came to a hotel, they were greeted by a woman in man's clothing introducing herself as the owner. When she turned her head and called one employee for help, out came a man in women's clothing. Although he was a tall guy with moustache in his face, he walked in mincing steps, talked in a thin voice, and even wore powder and rouge in his face! Tang Ao and his friends found this so strange and outlandish.

Gradually, Tang Ao and his friends got to know that this place was called the Kingdom of Women where female ran the official administration work. Women worked outside, while men stayed home taking care of household chores. After Tang Ao and his friends sold goods several days in the street, someone came to them and said, "Your jewelry and cosmetics are very good. Our king wants to buy some for her court ladies. Come with me to the palace to discuss the price."

Unexpectedly, as soon as the female king saw Lin Zhiyang, she took a liking to him and ordered him to become one of her "concubines" disregarding his protest. In no time a big crowd of "court ladies" came to change Lin Zhiyang's clothing. They put on decoration flowers in his hair and brushed rouge in his face. Seeing that his ears were not pierced, someone immediately picked up a needle and pierced two holes in his earlobes. Another one, finding his feet not bound, grabbed two stripes of cloth and bound his feet tightly. Lin Zhiyang couldn't walk with bound feet and felt the pain simply unbearable. He secretly grabbed a pair of scissors and cut loose from the foot wrap. Hearing this, the king was furious. "How can it be if you cannot follow the rules!" She reprimanded him. She ordered someone to flog Lin Zhiyang heavily with a board and confined him in a room, planning to marry him in several days.

Tang Ao and Duojiu Gong returned to their hotel and thought very hard. Finally, they came up with an idea. The rule went as before the marriage, the bride couldn't live in her husband's home. So, they said to the king, "Lin Zhiyang must live with us in the hotel. Come and take him to the palace when you are ready for the wedding ceremony." The king agreed, but sent many people to guard the hotel.

At night in the dark, Tang Ao and Duojiu Gong put Lin Zhiyang who was black and blue all over on their back and escaped the guards. Running out of the hotel in a hurry, they got on board of their

ship and fled this eccentric Kingdom of Women.

(Adapted from excerpts from *Flowers in the Mirror* by Li Ruzhen)

The Kingdom of Gentilities Written by Li Ruzhen

The Kingdom of Gentilities is a place where people are very courteous who don't argue with others, cherishing decorum and joyfulness. The king orders his people not to give officials any gifts. Anyone violating the rule of no gifting will be punished. The prime minister is very amiable and easy to approach, winning much affection and respect from his people. The people behave and talk very politely, yielding the right of way to each other in the road; businessmen sell high quality goods yet ask for low prices while customers insist on paying higher prices, each wanting the other party to gain more profit, thus making it hard to close a deal. The author conveys his ideal of life in the imaginary Kindom of Gentilities and expresses his dissatisfaction with the bullying and trickery in the real world and society.

Brief Introduction of the Work

Flowers in the Mirror is an open-minded and imaginative novel written by the novelist Li Ruzhen (1763—1830) in Qing Dynasty. It tells the story of Tang Ao, a scholar, and his friends, Lin Zhiyang and Duojiu Gong, who went overseas to do business when Wu Zetian was the emperor. One of the stories inside the book is *The Kingdom of Women*. In the Kingdom of Women, men managed the household affairs and women took charge of the state affairs. From the emperor to the ministers, all of them were women. In a humorous way the author questions the superiority of men over women.

The Female Emperor of China—Wu Zetian

Was there a female emperor in Chinese history? The answer is Yes, and her name was Wu Zetian (624—705), who was originally a queen in the Tang Dynasty, but later became the emperor and changed the name of her empire to "Zhou". She invented the Chinese character "曌" as her name, which means "the sun and the moon shine above the sky and light up the land". She reigned the country many years, during which time the society was stable, the population increased, and agriculture, handicrafts, and commerce all developed. When Wu Zetian was the emperor, she also had female officials. She put people in official posts basing on their ability rather than their family background, which made her a remarkable female politician in ancient China.

第三课

草船借箭（上）

诸葛亮是个才智过人的军师，周瑜一直对他不服气，总是刁难他。

这天，周瑜派人把诸葛亮请来，装作请教的样子，问他："先生，再过几天，我们就要和曹军打仗了，水陆交战，用什么兵器最好呢？"诸葛亮说："当然是弓箭好了。"周瑜一听，连忙说："先生和我想的一样。不过我军缺少弓箭，想请先生负责赶造十万支箭。打曹操是我们孙、刘两家的事，希望先生不要推辞。"诸葛亮说："好说，好说。都督派我做这件事，我一定尽力。只是不知道您什么时候要用这些箭？"周瑜说："你看十天完成，怎么样？"诸葛亮说："曹操大军很快要进攻我们，如果花费十天时间造箭，恐怕会误事。"

诸葛亮

周瑜

周瑜急忙又问:"那你说几天能完成呢?"诸葛亮伸出三个手指,对周瑜说:"三天之后,十万支箭送给都督。"三天造出十万支箭,这是根本不可能的。周瑜一听,立刻板起脸说:"先生和我开玩笑吗?"诸葛亮说:"军中无戏言,我愿和都督签下生死文书。如果三天造不出十万支箭,你可以砍我的头。"周瑜一听,心中大喜,当时就和诸葛亮签下了生死文书。诸葛亮说:"今天来不及了,明天开始造。三天以后,请都督派五百士兵到江边取箭。"

诸葛亮离开后,周瑜手下的人都奇怪地问:"三天怎么能造出十万支箭?诸葛亮是不是在骗我们?"周瑜说:"是他自己送死,不是我逼他的。如果到时候造不出来,我就定他死罪。"

当天,周瑜派手下鲁肃去诸葛亮那里探听情况。鲁肃是诸葛亮的好朋友,他很为诸葛亮担心。

诸葛亮见鲁肃来了,就说:"周瑜明明是刁难我。十万支箭,三天哪儿能造好?您一定要救我呀。"鲁肃说:"是你自己说大话,我怎么救你?"诸葛亮说:"请你帮我一个忙:借给我二十条船,每条船上有三十个士兵。这些船,全都用黑布蒙好,还要有一千个稻草人,安放在船舱的两边,我自有妙用。这些秘密,请您千万不要对都督说起。"

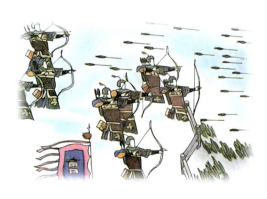

草船借箭

生词

zhū gě liàng 诸葛亮	Zhuge Liang (name)	wù shì 误事	hold matters up
cái zhì 才智	wit	qiān 签	sign
zhōu yú 周瑜	Zhou Yu (name)	lǔ sù 鲁肃	Lu Su (name)
diāo nàn 刁难	create difficulties	tàn tīng 探听	snoop, inquire
quē shǎo 缺少	lack of	méng 蒙	cover
fù zé 负责	repsonsible for	ān fàng 安放	put
tuī cí 推辞	decline	chuán cāng 船舱	cabin
dū du 都督	military commander	mì mì 秘密	secret
huā fei 花费	spend		
kǒng pà 恐怕	be afraid		

听写

才智　刁难　缺少　负责　花费　恐怕　误事　签

探听　安放　船舱　秘密

比一比

误 { 误事 / 错误 }

秘 { 秘密 / 神秘 / 秘书 }

舱 { 船舱 / 客舱 }

签 { 签名 / 签字 }

| 必 | 秘 |

<u>必</u>须　　　<u>秘</u>密

组词游戏

借

借船——借书——借钱——借车——借房子

借住——借笔——借用——借光——借衣服

反义词

推辞——接受　　　刁难——宽容

秘密——公开

多音字

难 {nàn: 刁难, 难民}   难 {nán: 难受, 难听}

词语运用

负责

① 我们小组出去爬山，我负责照相。

② 与曹操交战，诸葛亮负责造十万支箭。

③ 周小亮对工作很负责。

恐怕

① 燕子低飞，蚂蚁搬家，恐怕要下雨了。

② 你现在才去机场，恐怕赶不上飞机了。

③ 电影8点开始，我们再不走，恐怕就来不及了。

花费

① 这次去欧洲的旅行，花费不少。

② 姐姐在滑冰运动上花费了许多时间。

③ 他花费了许多精力学习中国功夫。

词语解释

军师——古代官名。

军中无戏言——军队中讨论作战时，不可以开玩笑。

生死文书——一种完不成任务，自愿受死的保证书。

说大话——话说得过分，超过实际才能。

自有妙用——自然有巧妙的用处。

思考题

诸葛亮为什么向鲁肃借船，又不让他告诉周瑜？

资料

作品简介

《三国演义》是中国古代优秀的长篇历史小说。作者罗贯(guàn)中是元末明初人（约1330—约1400）。《三国演义》描写了东汉末年和三国时期曹操、刘备、孙权(quán)三者之间在军事、政治、外交等方面的斗争。作者笔下的战争充满了斗智斗勇的精彩情节，其中"草船借箭""借东风"等故事生动、神奇，广为流传。诸葛亮是全书的中心人物之一，他具有杰出的智慧(huì)和非凡的军事指挥才能，在中国人的心目中已成为智慧的化身。

本文人物

诸葛亮：西蜀(shǔ)刘备的军师　　周瑜：东吴孙权的都督

鲁肃：东吴大臣，诸葛亮的朋友　　曹操：汉朝丞(chéng)相

Lesson Three

Borrow Arrows with Thatched Boats (I)

Zhuge Liang was an outstandingly wise military strategist. Zhou Yu was unconvinced of his talents and had always been creating difficulties for him.

One day, Zhou Yu sent someone to get Zhuge Liang to his tent, pretending to ask for his advice, "Sir, in a few days we are going to combat with the army of Cao Cao. What weapon is the best for such a battle in land and water?" "The best weapon is certainly bows and arrows," answered Zhuge Liang. As soon as Zhou Yu heard this, he said, "I have exactly the same idea as yours, but our army are short of arrows. I want to ask you to take the responsibility of making 100,000 arrows as soon as possible. Fighting Cao Cao is the task for both Sun and Liu administration. I hope you sir will not decline this job." Zhuge Liang said, "No problem, no problem. Since you, Commander-in-Chief, allot to me this task, I will certainly do my best. I just want to know when you need these arrows." Zhou Yu answered, "How about in ten days?" Zhuge Liang said, "Cao Cao's army will soon attack us. I am afraid waiting for ten days will be too late. "

Zhou Yu asked hastily, "Then you tell me. How many days can you complete the task?" Zhuge Liang put forward three fingers, saying to Zhou Yu, "In three days, I will give Commander-in-Chief 100,000 arrows." It's absolutely impossible to make 100,000 arrows in three days. Hearing this, Zhou Yu put on a straight face and said, "Sir, are you telling me a joke?" Zhuge Liang said, "There is no jest in war. I can sign a life waiver with Commander-in-chief. If I cannot make 100,000 arrows in three days, you can cut off my head." Zhou Yu was very pleased to hear this and immediately signed the life waiver with Zhuge Liang on the spot. Zhuge Liang said, "It is too late today. I will start from tomorrow. In three days from tomorrow, sir, you can send 500 soldiers to the riverside to get the arrows."

After Zhuge Liang left, the subordinates of Zhou Yu all asked in surprise, "How can it be possible to make 100,000 arrows in three days? Can Zhuge Liang be kidding us?" Zhou Yu said, "Then his death is proposed by himself, not forced by me. If he cannot make them, I will sentence him to death."

On that day, Zhou Yu sent his subordinate Lu Su to Zhuge Liang to inquire the situation. Being Zhuge Liang's good friend, Lu Su was very worried for Zhuge Liang.

Seeing Lu Su come, Zhuge Liang said, "Zhou Yu obviously was creating troubles for me. One hundred thousand arrows! How can they be made in three days? You must save me." Lu Su said, "It's you yourself who bragged. How can I save you?" Zhuge Liang said, "Please give me a big favor. Lend me 20 boats. Put on board each boat 30 soldiers. Cover the boats with black cloths. Set 1,000 scarecrows on both sides of the boats. I have my good use of them. These are all secrets. Please don't tell the Commander-in- Chief."

Brief Introduction of the work

The Romance of the Three Kingdoms is an excellent historical novel of ancient China. The author, Luo Guanzhong, lived in the late Yuan and early Ming Dynasties (c. 1330 - 1400). *The Romance of the Three Kingdoms* depicts the battles on levels of military, politics, and diplomacy among Cao Cao, Liu Bei, and Sun Quan in the late Eastern Han Dynasty and the Three Kingdoms Period. The author describes the wars with exciting episodes displaying wisdom and courage, among which the stories of "Borrow Arrows with Thatched Boats" and "Borrow the East Wind" were especially vivid and magical, and had been widely circulated. The central character of the book, Zhuge Liang, with his outstanding wisdom and extraordinary military command skills, is the embodiment of wisdom in the minds of Chinese people.

The main characters in this lesson

Zhuge Liang: military advisor of Liu Bei in Western Shu
Zhou Yu: governor of Sun Quan in Eastern Wu
Lu Su: minister of Eastern Wu, friend of Zhuge Liang
Cao Cao: prime minister of Han Dynasty

第四课

草船借箭（下）

鲁肃不知道诸葛亮借船有什么用，但还是答应了。回去见到周瑜，他果然没提借船的事。鲁肃私自派了二十条快船，按照诸葛亮说的，用黑布把船蒙好，船上安上稻草人，等候诸葛亮调用。

第一天，不见诸葛亮的动静；第二天，还不见诸葛亮的动静；直到第三天的深夜，诸葛亮突然跑来找鲁肃，对鲁肃说："我请您和我一起去取箭。"说着，拉着鲁肃就上船。鲁肃问："到哪里取？"诸葛亮说："不用问，去了就知道了。"

诸葛亮吩咐用绳子把二十条船一一连接起来，悄悄地朝江北岸划去。这时候，江上起了大雾，几丈之外就看不见人影了。大约五点钟时，船队已靠近曹军水寨。诸葛亮命令士兵把船一字排开，又叫船上的士兵一边敲鼓，一边大声叫喊。他和鲁肃却坐

草船借箭　　　　　　　　　　　　　刘艺　画

在船舱中喝酒。鲁肃吃惊地问:"咱们人这么少,如果曹军冲过来,怎么办?"诸葛亮笑着说:"这样大的雾,曹军又不熟悉水战,他们怎么敢派兵出来?您就放心继续喝酒吧。"

曹操听到鼓声和喊声,以为敌人进攻了。他刚要下令出兵,又一想,江上这么大的雾,敌人一定有埋伏,不该出去迎战。于是传令说:"江上雾太大,不要轻易出动。多派弓箭手向敌人射箭,不要让他们靠近。"

曹操派了一万弓箭手来到江边,他们一齐放箭。几十万支箭连续飞出,好像下雨一样射到船上。只过了一会儿,船一侧的稻草人身上就插满了箭。诸葛亮又下令掉转船头,让船的另一侧对着曹军,仍旧让士兵敲鼓喊叫。很快,船另一侧的稻草人上也插满了曹军射来的箭。

太阳出来了,江面上的雾慢慢散去。只见二十条船两侧的稻草人身上全都插满了箭。诸葛亮一见,大功告成,就下令快速开船返回,又让士兵齐声大喊:"谢曹丞相送箭!"等到曹操明白上当了,诸葛亮的船早已开出二十多里,追也来不及了。

二十条船靠岸的时候,周瑜派来的五百士兵正好前来取箭。每条船上大约五六千支箭,二十条船总共有十万多支。

鲁肃把诸葛亮借箭的经过告诉了周瑜,周瑜长叹一声,说:"诸葛亮神机妙算,我真不如他。"

(根据罗贯中著《三国演义》选段改编)

生 词

sī zì 私自	privately, secretly	mái fu 埋伏	ambush
diào yòng 调用	transfer temporarily	yíng zhàn 迎战	fight against
dòng jing 动静	activity	hǎo xiàng 好像	be like, seem
fēn fu 吩咐	instruct	chā mǎn 插满	full of
huá 划	row	réng jiù 仍旧	still
kào jìn 靠近	close to	sàn qù 散去	disperse
shuǐ zhài 水寨	military base in water	dà gōng gào chéng 大功告成	be accomplished
qiāo gǔ 敲鼓	pound on the drums	chéng xiàng 丞相	prime minister
shú xi 熟悉	be familiar with	shén jī miào suàn 神机妙算	have clever strategy and shrewed tactics

听 写

私自　调用　动静　划　敲鼓　熟悉　埋伏　迎战

插满　仍旧　散去　大功告成　*神机妙算

比一比

划 { 划船 / 计划 }　　　　寨 { 水寨 / 山寨 }

散 { 散开 / 散场 }　　　　派 { 派人 / 派老师 }

| 奶 | 仍 | 扔 |

奶奶　　仍旧　　扔东西

组词游戏

私

私人——私车——私自——私下——自私——私心

私立学校——私立医院——私人秘书——私人飞机

反义词

敌人——朋友　　　　神机妙算——毫无办法

多音字

huá	huà
划	划
划船	计划

词语运用

派

① 马上要出发了，林华还没到，老师派班长去找他。

② 与曹操大战之前，周瑜派诸葛亮造十万支箭。

③ 公司派爸爸到上海工作。

仍旧

① 这么多年没见到姑姑，这次相见，她仍旧那么年轻。

② 现在弟弟已经是高中生了，他仍旧喜欢养小动物。

③ 第一天诸葛亮没有动静，第二天诸葛亮仍旧没有动静。

词语解释

丈——长度单位,约为3.33米。

轻易——简单、容易;随随便便。

连续——接连的。

思考题

诸葛亮取箭的时候,怎么正好天下大雾?

阅读

草船借箭（课本剧）

人物：诸葛亮、周瑜、鲁肃、士兵甲、士兵乙

旁　　白：诸葛亮是一个才智过人的军师，周瑜对他一直不服气，总是刁难他。

　　　　　周瑜带着士兵甲出场，诸葛亮另一边出场，见面相互作揖(yī)行礼

周　　瑜：先生，再过几天，我们就要和曹军打仗了，水陆交战用什么兵器最好呢？

诸葛亮：当然是弓箭好了。

周　　瑜：先生和我想的一样，不过我军缺少弓箭，想请先生负责造十万支箭。希望先生不要推辞。

诸葛亮：好说，好说。什么时候用这些箭？

周　　瑜：十天完成怎么样？

诸葛亮：曹操大军很快要进攻我们，花费十天造箭，恐怕会误事。

周　　瑜：那你说几天能完成呢？

诸葛亮：（伸出三个手指）三天之后送给都督。

周　　瑜：（板起脸）先生和我开玩笑吗？

诸葛亮：军中无戏言，我愿签下生死文书。三天造不出十万支箭，可以砍我的头。三天之后，请派五百人到江边取箭。

旁　　白：周瑜一听，心中大喜，当时就和诸葛亮立下了生死文书。

　　　　　诸葛亮离场

周　　瑜：是他自己送死，不是我逼他。到时候造不出箭，我就定他死罪。

周瑜及手下人离场

旁　　白：当天，周瑜派鲁肃去诸葛亮那里探听情况。鲁肃是诸葛亮的好朋友，他很担心。

诸葛亮先上场，之后鲁肃急急忙忙上场

诸葛亮：周瑜明明是要刁难我，十万支箭三天哪能造好？你一定要救我呀。

鲁　肃：是你自己说大话，我怎么救你？

诸葛亮：请借我二十条船，用黑布蒙好，每条船上三十个士兵。还要一千个稻草人，放在船舱的两边，我自有妙用，这些不要对都督说起。

旁　　白：鲁肃答应了。把船和稻草人都准备好了。

第一天，第二天，诸葛亮都没有动静。

第三天深夜，诸葛亮突然跑来找鲁肃。

诸葛亮：我们一起去取箭。

旁　　白：诸葛亮叫人用绳子把二十条船连起来。朝曹操水寨划去。这时江上起了大雾，几丈之外就看不见人了。诸葛亮命令把船一字排开，又叫士兵敲鼓、喊叫。（鼓声）

鲁　肃：我们人少，曹军冲出来怎么办？

诸葛亮：这么大的雾，他们不敢派兵出来，我们喝酒吧。

士兵乙：曹丞相令，江上雾大，不可出兵，派一万弓箭手向敌人射箭！

旁　　白：曹军弓箭手一齐放箭。箭像下雨一样射到船上。不久船上的稻草人插满了箭。

太阳出来了，雾散去。诸葛亮下令返回。让士兵喊："谢曹丞相送箭！"

诸葛亮离场，周瑜、士兵甲出场，鲁肃在一旁

士兵甲：报告都督，箭共十万多支。

周　瑜：（听鲁肃讲了借箭经过，长叹一声）诸葛亮神机妙算，我真不如他。

Lesson Four

Borrow Arrows with Thatched Boats (II)

Although Lu Su didn't know what Zhuge Liang was going to do with the boats, he agreed to lend them to him. He kept his promise and didn't tell Zhou Yu about lending boats to Zhuge Liang when he reported to Zhou Yu after the visit. Lu Su lent Zhuge Liang in private twenty clippers which were all covered with black cloths, lined with scarecrows on both sides, according to Zhuge Liang's requirement, ready to be put in use by Zhuge Liang.

On the first day, Zhuge Liang did nothing; on the second day, still nothing; until the night of the third day, Zhuge Liang suddenly came to Lu Su and said, "I come to ask you to get the arrows together with me." he grabbed Lu Su's hand while speaking and got on board a boat. "Where do we get the arrows?" Lu Su asked. "Don't ask. You will know when you get there."

Zhuge Liang asked the soldiers to connect the twenty boats with ropes. Quietly the boats were rowed towards the north side of the Yangze River. At that time, heavy fog began to roll up on the river. Nothing could be seen a few away. At around 5 am, the fleet of boats were near the area of water where Cao Cao's army stayed. Zhuge Liang ordered the soldiers to line up the boats in a row. After that, he ordered them to beat the drums and shout loudly. He and Lu Su stayed inside the cabin and drank wine. Lu Su was astonished and asked him, "We have so few soldiers. What shall we do if Cao's army rush over to us?" Zhuge Liang replied with laughter, "The fog is so heavy, and Cao Cao's army is not familiar with water battle. How dare he send troops out? You relax and continue drinking."

Hearing the drumming and shouting, Cao Cao thought the enemy was attacking. He was just about to order the troops out, but then thought, "The river is so foggy. The enemy must have an ambush. I should not let the army go out to fight the battle." So, he sent out this order, "It is too foggy on the river. Don't go out rashly. Send more archers to shoot arrows at the enemy. Don't let them get close."

Cao Cao sent to the river bank 10,000 archers who shot arrows in unison. Hundreds of thousands of arrows were shot out continuously like rain drops falling onto the boats of Zhuge Liang. In a short while, the scarecrows on one side of the boats were full of arrows. Zhuge Liang ordered the boats to turn around so the other side was towards Cao Cao's army. Very soon, the scarecrows on the other side of the boats were also full of arrows shot by Cao Cao's army.

The sun rose up; the fog on the river dissipated gradually. The scarecrows on both sides of the boats were full of arrows. Seeing this, Zhuge Liang knew the task was successfully accomplished. He quickly ordered the boats to sail back in full speed, and let the soldiers shout out "Thank you, Prime Minister Cao, for giving us arrows!" When Cao Cao realized that he was tricked, Zhuge Liang's boats had sailed too far away to be caught up with.

Right at the time when the twenty boats docked, the five hundred soldiers sent by Zhou Yu came to collect the arrows. Each boat had about five or six thousand arrows, and the twenty boats had a total of more than 100,000 arrows.

Lu Su told Zhou Yu about how Zhuge Liang borrowed the arrows. Zhou Yu sighed long and hard, saying, "Zhuge Liang has the divine strategy and shrewd calculation. I am really not his equal."

(Adapted from an excerpt from *Romance of the Three Kingdoms* by Luo Guanzhong)

第五课

孙悟空三打白骨精

这天,唐僧师徒四人来到一座大山前。唐僧饿了,悟空跳到云端一望,对唐僧说:"这里是深山野谷,没有人家,只有一片桃林,我去摘些桃子给您吃。"他让八戒、沙僧好好儿保护师父,就直奔桃林而去。

不想这山里有一个妖精,看见唐僧,心中欢喜:"运气,运气!早就听说有个去西天取经的唐僧,谁吃他一块肉,就能长生不老。今天他果然来了。"可是八戒、沙僧守在旁边,一时无法下手。妖精想了一个办法,她摇身一变,变成一个年轻女子,提着罐子朝唐僧走来。

八戒见一位年轻女子走来,连忙上前细声问道:"女菩萨,请问手里提的是什么东西?"妖精说:"罐子里是香米饭,给长老送的饭。"唐僧却问道:"女菩萨,你家住哪里?为什么要给和尚送饭呢?"妖精编假话说:"我家住在山下,原是给丈夫送饭,不想遇到长老,这饭就敬长老吧。"唐僧说:"多谢了!我徒弟去摘桃子了,一会儿就回来,我们要是吃了你的饭,你丈

夫就没有饭吃了。"这下可急坏了猪八戒，他埋怨说："天下的和尚多得很，没有一个像师父这样不知好歹。现成的饭，三个人不吃，等那猴子回来就得分成四份了。"不由分说，拿起罐子就要吃。

正在这时，悟空拿着桃子回来了。他一眼就看出这女子是个妖精，举起棒子，当头就打！唐僧忙上前拦住说："不要随便伤人！"悟空说："师父，她是妖精，不要上当。"悟空又是一棒，那妖精也有办法，留下一个假尸，自己化成一阵清风逃走了。唐僧看看罐子，哪里有香米饭，全是绿皮青蛙！可八戒说："哥哥棍子重，打死了她，怕您念紧箍咒，故意用这个法子骗我们。"唐僧相信了八戒的话，念起了紧箍咒。孙悟空大叫："头疼！师父别念了，有话好说！"唐僧生气地说："如果再伤人，就念二十遍。""三十遍也由你，我以后不打人了。"悟空说。

再说那妖精见唐僧、猪八戒没认出她来，又摇身变成一个老太太，哭着走了过来。八戒说："师父，不好了，老妈妈找女儿来了。"悟空见那老婆婆又是妖精变的，便把师父念紧箍咒的事忘得一干二净，举棒就打。那妖精化成清风逃走，留下假尸。唐僧见了，气得二话不说，一连念了二十遍紧箍咒。悟空疼得在地上打滚，妖精看见暗自高兴。

唐僧师徒继续前行，走了不远看见一个老头儿，边走边念经。悟空看出又是妖精变的，他拔了根毫毛一吹，变成假悟空和妖精打，自己叫来山神、土地*一起打，那妖精无处可逃，被孙悟空打死在地。唐僧上前一看，原来是一堆白骨，上面有四个字"白骨夫人"，这才相信了悟空。可八戒挑拨说："师父，他打死了人，又使法子骗我们。"唐僧又信了八戒的话，赶悟空走。悟空说："师父错怪了我，那明明是个妖怪，一心想害你。你却听那呆子的胡言乱语，好坏不分。"悟空见唐僧怎么也不留他，只好含泪拜别了师父，一个筋斗回到了花果山，做起了自由自在的美猴王来。

（根据吴承恩（chéng ēn）著《西游记》选段改编）

---

* 山神、土地：传说中管理一个地方的山和土地的神仙。

生词

wù 悟	enlighten	fèn 份	portion
sēng 僧	monk	bàng zi 棒子	stick
zhāi 摘	pick	lán zhù 拦住	stop, hold back
jiè 戒	commandment	suí biàn 随便	at random, wantonly
yāo jing 妖精	demon, goblin	jiǎ shī 假尸	fake corpse
yùn qi 运气	fortune, luck	jǐn gū zhòu 紧箍咒	Band-tightening spell
pú sà 菩萨	bodhisattva	háo máo 毫毛	hair
tú di 徒弟	disciple, apprentice	tiǎo bō 挑拨	incite, provoke
mán yuàn 埋怨	complain	dāi zi 呆子	idiot
bù zhī hǎo dǎi 不知好歹	not to know good from bad	jīn dǒu 筋斗	somersault

听写

孙悟空　唐僧　摘　猪八戒　妖精　运气　菩萨

徒弟　埋怨　棒子　随便　假尸　挑拨　呆子

*不知好歹　毫毛　筋斗

比一比

随 { 随便 / 随时 / 随着 }　　　摘 { 摘桃 / 摘花 / 摘下来 }

{ 拨（挑拨）/ 泼（活泼）}　　　戒 { 戒烟 / 戒指 }

发	泼	拨
头发	活泼	挑拨

反义词

举起——放下　　　松——紧

暗自高兴——垂头丧气

多音字

tiǎo
挑

挑拨

tiāo
挑

挑水

děi	dé
得	得
děi 就得	dé 得到

词语运用

随便

① 今天吃自助餐，想吃什么随便拿。

② 上课不要随便说话，有问题请举手。

③ 老师说，教室里不能随便扔垃圾。

埋怨

① 这件事做错了只能怪自己，不能埋怨别人。

② 爷爷每天早起给我和妹妹做饭，从不埋怨。

③ 妈妈总是埋怨爸爸不关心孩子的教育。

词语解释

云端——云上，云中。

取经——本课意思是佛教徒到印度去求取佛经。

长老——对年长者的敬称，古代是对宗（zōng）教职（zhí）务高者的尊称。

上当——受骗。

暗自高兴——心里高兴但不表现出来。

思考题

1. 唐僧为什么爱听猪八戒的话？唐僧有优点吗？找一找。

2. 孙悟空是怎么对待猪八戒的？想一想。

3. 在你的小组中，你是如何对待有缺点的领导和队友？

分析唐僧取经的四人团队

| 火眼金睛 勇敢担当 | 人妖不分 糊涂善良 | 好吃懒做 挑拨是非 | 吃苦耐劳 默默付出 |

提示：

- 唐僧，是师父。他时常糊涂，人妖不分，让人无奈。
- 孙悟空，是大师兄。他神通广大，机智勇敢，常被师父错怪。
- 猪八戒，是二师兄。他一身毛病，好吃懒做、挑拨是非，但打妖怪也出力。
- 沙僧，是三师弟。他是好群众，打妖怪很出力。

(快板)

三打白骨精

唐僧西天去取经，
师徒四人向前行。
走到一座大山下，
山里有个白骨精。
早就想吃唐僧肉，
长生不老永年轻。

她趁悟空去摘桃，
变成女子把饭送。
不想悟空返回来，
当头一棒打妖精。
妖精化成一阵风，
留下假尸骗唐僧。

唐僧念起紧箍咒，
疼得悟空直喊停！
师父，师父，别念了！
我不打人啦，还不行？

唐僧错怪孙悟空，
妖怪看到心高兴。

摇身变成老太太，
喊着女儿哭不停。
悟空看出是妖精，
金箍棒下不留情。

妖怪逃走化成风，
又留假尸吓唐僧。
唐僧糊涂分不清，
八戒一旁扇冷风。

妖怪这次变老头儿，
口里喃喃念着经。
悟空招来土地神，
围着打死白骨精。
一堆白骨在眼前，
"白骨夫人"白骨精！
唐僧这才如梦醒。
这故事就叫：孙悟空三打白骨精！

资　料

作品简介

《西游记》是中国明代的一部小说，作者吴承恩（约1500—约1582）。书中讲述了唐僧和徒弟孙悟空、猪八戒、沙和尚去西天取经的故事。

孙悟空是《西游记》中的主要人物。他是一位神话英雄，也是人们喜爱的美猴王。他神通广大，会七十二种变化；他机智勇敢，什么都不怕，打败了一路上碰到的妖精，保护唐僧到达西天，取到了真经。

《西游记》是中国少年儿童喜爱阅读的古典小说之一。

English Translation

Lesson Five

Sun Wukong Hits Thrice the White-Bone Demon

One day, Tang Seng and his three disciples came to a big mountain. Tang Seng felt hungry. Wukong jumped up to the cloud and looked around, telling Tang Seng, "It's a wild valley with no households around. There is only a patch of peach trees. I will go and fetch some peaches for you to eat." He asked Bajie and Sha Seng to well guard the master and went straightly to the peach forest.

It happened that there lived a demon in the mountain. It was very happy to see Tang Seng, "Lucky me! Lucky me! I have long ago heard that there is a monk from Tang who is going to the West to fetch the scriptures. Whoever eats one piece of his flesh can live and stay young forever. Today he really comes!" But with Bajie and Sha Seng beside Tang Seng, it couldn't get him. Then the demon came up with an idea. It transformed into a young woman holding a jar and walked towards Tang Seng.

Seeing a young woman walking near, Bajie hurried up and asked softly, "Lady Bodhisattva, may I know what you are holding in your hands?" The demon answered, "In the jar is some aromatic rice which is my offering to the master." However, Tang Seng asked her, "Lady Bodhisattva, where is your home? Why do you offer a meal to me?" The demon told a lie, saying, "I live at the foot of the mountain. I originally was bringing the meal to my husband. But now I see you, the venerable, I want to offer it to you, venerable master. " Tang Seng answered, "Thank you a lot! But my disciple went to pick peaches for me. He will return in a minute. If we eat the meal, your husband won't have anything to eat." Zhu Bajie was unhappy to hear this and complained, "There are many monks in the world but none is like my master who doesn't know what is good or bad. There is a ready meal for the three of us. If we don't eat it now, when the monkey comes back, there will be four to share it. " Allowing no more discussion he took the jar and was about to start eating.

Right at that moment, Wukong returned with peaches. At a single glance he knew the woman was a demon. He lifted his cudgel and was going to hit it on the head, but Tang Seng rushed forward and blocked him, saying, "Don't harm people so carelessly!" Wukong said, "Master, she is a demon. Don't be fooled." He hurled the cudgel upon the demon who changed into a breeze and fled away, leaving a fake corpse on the ground. Looking into the jar, Tang Seng saw no rice but a bunch of green skinned frogs. But Bajie said, "Master, Brother's heavy cudgel killed the female Bodhisattva. He is afraid that you will chant the Tightening-crown Spell, so he tricked us with this." Believing these words by Bajie, Tang Seng began to chant the Tightening-crown spell. Sun Wukong yelled, "My head aches! Master, stop it. We can discuss this." Tang Seng spoke indignantly, "If you harm another person, I will chant twenty times." "You can chant thirty times. I won't beat people anymore." Wukong said.

Now that the demon saw Tang Seng and Zhu Bajie didn't see through it, it changed into an old woman walking towards them who cried along the way. Bajie said, "Craps! Master! The old woman is now looking for her daughter." Wukong saw through the old woman and knew it was the transformed demon again. He completely forgot about that Tang Seng might chant the Tightening-crown spell and hit it instantly with his cudgel. The demon fled again in a wind, leaving behind a fake corpse. Extremely angry at seeing the corpse, without saying a word, Tang Seng chanted twenty times the Tightening-crown spell in one breath. Wukong rolled on the ground with pain. The demon was very happy to see this in the dark.

Tang Seng and his disciples continued to walk. In not too far they saw an old man chanting sutra while walking. Wukong saw it was the demon again. He plucked a hair and with a blow turned it into a fake Wukong fighting with the demon; in the meantime, he called out the god of the mountain and the master of the land to fight together. This time, having nowhere to escape, the demon was finally killed by Sun Wukong on the ground. Tang Seng walked forward and saw a pile of white bones on which there were four words-The White Bone Lady. Only by then did he believe Sun Wukong. But Bajie provoked him on purpose by saying, "Master, he killed people but fooled us by tricks." Tang Seng believed Bajie again and dismissed Wukong. Wukong said to him, "Master! You blame me unjustly! That was obviously a demon bent on harming you. But you would rather listen to that fool's nonsense, making no distinction between good and bad." Seeing that Tangseng wouldn't let him stay, Wukong tearfully bid farewell to the master. With one somersault, he went back to the Mountain of Flowers and Fruits, and resumed the free and easy life of Monkey King.

(Adapted from excerpts from *Journey to the West* by Wu Cheng'en)

Brief Introduction of the Work

Journey to the West is a Chinese novel from the Ming Dynasty by Wu Chengen (c. 1500-1582).

The book tells the story of Tang Seng and his disciples Sun Wukong, Zhu Bajie and Sha Heshang who go to the West Heaven to get scriptures.

Sun Wukong, the mythical hero and popular Monkey King, is the main character in *Journey to the West*. He is so powerful that he can perform seventy-two transformation; so wise and brave that he fears nothing. He defeats all the demons he encounters along the way to protect Tang Seng who reaches the Western Paradise and gets the true scriptures.

Journey to the West is one of the popular classical novels for Chinese children.

第六课

陋室铭

[唐]刘禹锡(xī)

　　山不在高,有仙则名。水不在深,有龙则灵。斯是陋室,唯吾德馨。苔痕上阶绿,草色入帘青。谈笑有鸿儒,往来无白丁。可以调素琴,阅金经。无丝竹之乱耳,无案牍之劳形。南阳诸葛庐,西蜀子云亭。

　　孔子云:"何陋之有?"

【译文】

　　山不在于高低，只要有神仙就是名山。水不在于深浅，只要有龙便有灵气。这虽是一处简陋的房子，我的美德却远近闻名。绿苔爬上石阶，青草映入门帘。谈笑好友是饱学之士，没有不学无术之人。这儿可以弹弹琴，读读经。远离闹市嘈杂，更无公文劳身。如同诸葛亮的草屋，扬雄的草亭。孔子说过："这哪里是简陋呢？"

【注释】

　　铭：古代刻于金石上的一种押韵文体。

　　斯：这个。

　　德馨：德，品德；馨，美好。

　　苔痕上阶绿：台阶上长满绿苔。

　　草色入帘青：门前满是鲜翠的青草。

　　素琴：不加雕饰的琴。

徐雨亭　画

丝竹：音乐，这是暗指官场上聚会。

案牍：官府文书。案，办公桌；牍，古代写字用的木片，指文件、书信。

鸿儒：博学多闻的儒者。

白丁：不学无术之人。

南阳诸葛庐：诸葛亮的住所。

西蜀子云亭：扬雄隐居的住所。

生词

陋室 lòu shì	humble room	帘 lián	curtain
铭 míng	epigraph, inscription	鸿儒 hóng rú	learned scholar
斯 sī	this	案牍 àn dú	official correspondence
吾 wú	I	庐 lú	dwelling place
苔痕 tái hén	moss	蜀 shǔ	the kingdom of Shu Han

听写

陋室　铭　斯　吾　苔痕　帘　鸿儒　案牍　庐　蜀

（或：背诵、默写全文）

比一比

陋 { 陋室 / 丑陋 }　　帘 { 窗帘 / 门帘 }　　{ 读（读书）/ 牍（案牍）}

需
需要

儒
儒生

组词游戏

案

案件——案子——案牍——档案——学习方案

教学方案——作战方案——环保方案——治疗方案

反义词

简陋——精致/豪华　　鸿儒——白丁

阅读

手机铭

张智明：Benjamin Zhang（六年级）

屏不在大，方便就行。机不在快，好用则灵。

斯是轻小，用法无穷。

机身可折叠，屏幕能触摸。网上有朋友，还能看电影。

可以查资料，做作业。

无机身之沉重，无胳膊之酸痛。

苹果小手机，微软大程序。

孔子云："何陋之有？"

徐雨亭　画

资料

作者简介

刘禹锡（772—842）唐代著名文学家，与白居易齐名，著有《刘梦得文集》等。

 English Translation

Lesson six

An Epigraph in Praise of My Humble Home

Liu Yuxi (Tang Dynastry)

Mountains needn't be high;
They are famous if deities in them reside.
Waters needn't be deep;
They are magical if dragons live inside.
A simple dwelling this room is;
yet from it my virtue emanates fragrance.
On the doorsteps are the climbing green moss.
Through the curtain I see the green grass.
Learned scholars come to discuss and laugh with me;
I keep no ignorant people as company.
I can play my plain qin,
or read the Diamond Sutra.
No strings and pipes jar on my ears;
No official files exhaust my body.
My place is like the thatched hut of Zhuge Liang in Nanyang,
or the Pavilion Zhao Ziyun of West Shu once dwelled in.
Confucius once said, "What is anything humble about it?"

Epigraph to My Cell Phone

Zhang Zhiming (Grade Six)

The screen needn't be large as long as it is convenient.
The phone doesn't need to be speedy as long as it is easy to use.
Although it's light and small, its function is limitless.
The phone can be folded, and it has a touch screen.
On the Internet I have friends, and I can watch movies, google information, and do homework.
It's not heavy, so my arms won't get sour.
The Apple phone is small; the Microsoft system is huge.
Confucius said,
"What's simple about it?"

Brief Introduction of the Author

Liu Yuxi (772-842), was a famous literary figure in the Tang Dynasty. He was equally famous with Bai Juyi, and was the author of *Liu Mengde's Collected Works*, etc.

第七课

鸡毛信

故事发生在抗日战争时期。那一年海娃十四岁,是龙门村儿童团的团长。一天傍晚,海娃正在山上一边放羊,一边放哨。爸爸急急忙忙地跑来,拿出一封信,对海娃说:"马上去王庄,把信送给民兵队张队长。"海娃接过信一看,信上插着三根鸡毛,是一封很紧急的信。海娃收好信,赶着羊群就走了。

谁知走到山脚下,糟糕!海娃看见一队抢粮的日本兵。日本兵越走越近。海娃急了,把鸡毛信藏在哪儿呢?他看着胖乎乎的羊尾巴,心头一动,赶快抱住那只带头的老绵羊,把信绑在它的尾巴底下。海娃站起来,甩了一个响鞭,赶着羊群朝日本兵走过去。

"站住!"日本兵喊起来,"哗啦"一声,举起枪,对着海娃的脑袋。他们把海娃拉到日本军官面前。海娃故意歪着脑袋,张着大嘴,傻乎乎地望着他。他们把海娃全身搜了一遍,连两只

穿破的鞋也没放过，可是什么也没搜出来。他们不放海娃，让海娃赶着羊群跟着他们走。

太阳落山了，日本兵停在一个小村庄里，宰了几只羊烤羊肉吃。海娃顾不上心疼他的羊了，偷偷把手伸到老绵羊的大尾巴下面一摸，信还在呢！他放心了。日本兵吃饱了，抱着枪睡觉去了。他们让海娃睡在最里头。海娃睡不着，他想："日本兵明天还要宰羊，要是今晚跑不掉，鸡毛信可就完了。"他轻轻地迈过日本兵的大腿，跑出来抱住那只老绵羊把信解下来，放进口袋，一口气向山上跑去。

天亮了，海娃爬上山顶，看见山那头有个日本兵拿着小白旗朝着他来回摇晃。海娃脱下白布上衣，学着日本兵的样子也来回摇晃。没想到，真混过去了。他又跑到对面山顶，再走不远就是王庄啦，海娃高兴极了。他一屁股坐在山头上，手伸进口袋一摸，不觉浑身哆嗦起来。鸡毛信呢？口袋里没有啦。海娃把身边的石头缝都找了一遍，也没有。海娃马上往回跑，沿着来的路，一边跑一边找。他跑到摇晃衣服的地方，鸡毛信好好儿地躺在那儿。海娃高兴极了，把信装进口袋，刚想往回跑，没想到日本兵又赶来了，抓住海娃让他带路。

海娃赶着羊，在前面走。在山坡上，海娃把羊赶上了一条羊道。羊道越来越不好走。日本兵走走停停远远落在后面。日本兵吼道："慢慢的！"海娃不理他们，拼命往前跑。日本兵开枪了。海娃实在跑不动了,一头扑倒在乱草里。山顶上突然响起了一阵枪声,海娃听出来,是自己人的枪声……

等海娃睁开眼睛,看见的正是张队长。他问:"信——鸡毛信?"张队长摸着海娃的脑袋说:"放心吧,收到了。你把日本兵带到没路的地方,我们把敌人消灭了。谢谢你这个小英雄。"

生词

kàng rì zhàn zhēng 抗日战争	the War of Anti-Japanese Invasion	sōu 搜	search
ér tóng 儿童	children	cūn zhuāng 村庄	village
fàng shào 放哨	stand sentry	xīn téng 心疼	love dearly
jǐn jí 紧急	urgent	hùn 混	deceive, mislead
mián yáng 绵羊	sheep	duō suo 哆嗦	shiver
bǎng 绑	bind, tie	pīn mìng 拼命	exert the utmost strength
biān 鞭	whip, lash	xiāo miè 消灭	eliminate

听写

抗日战争　儿童　放哨　紧急　绑　鞭　搜

村庄　心疼　哆嗦　拼命　消灭　*绵羊

比一比

脑 { 脑袋 / 动脑 / 脑子好

消 { 消息 / 消灭

童 { 童（儿童）/ 撞（撞到）

{ 枪（手枪）/ 抢（抢粮）

| 傍 | 旁 | 饱 | 包 |

傍晚　　旁边　　吃饱　　书包

反义词

战争——和平　　儿童——成人

绑上——解开　　饱——饿

多音字

luò	là
落	落
落叶	丢三落四

词语运用

拼命

① 日本兵大叫："站住！"海娃拼命往前跑。

② 游泳比赛，每个运动员都拼命往前游。

③ 别看他个子小，干活可真拼命。

糟糕

① 糟糕，我的饭又煮糊了！

② 没有比今年更糟糕的了，全世界新冠肺炎流行。

③ 哥哥昨天撞了车，更糟糕的是，爸爸又丢了工作。

词语解释

儿童团——一般指抗日时期的儿童抗日组织。

羊道——羊走的路,非常细小,很难走。

阅读

雨来没有死

雨来12岁,家在芦(lú)花村。村边有条河,夏天雨来和小朋友像一群鱼,在河里钻上钻下。爸爸说不上学不行,叫雨来上了夜校。雨来的课本是用土纸油印的。雨来把书放在腿上,女老师教大家认字,念着:"我们是中国人,我们爱自己的祖国。"大家齐声轻轻地跟着念。

鬼子又"扫荡"了,爸爸离家打鬼子去了。这天,交通员李大叔跑进雨来家,街上有日本鬼子大声地叫喊。李大叔忙把墙角的缸搬开,下面有个洞,他跳进洞里,说:"雨来,把缸搬回去,对谁也不许说。"雨来把缸搬回去,他刚到堂屋,鬼子就冲进大门。鬼子问雨来:"刚才有个人跑进来,看见没有?"雨来说:"我在屋里,什么也没看见。"鬼子扭着雨来的两只耳朵,向两边拉,又打雨来,疼得他两眼冒(mào)金花,鼻子流血。鬼子打累了,气得叫:"拉出去,枪毙(bì)!"芦花村里的人听到河边响了几枪,人们都哭了。

鬼子走后,人们来到河边。啊!水面上露出个小脑袋,扒着芦苇(wěi)问:"鬼子走了?""雨来没有死!"大家高兴地喊。原来枪响以前,雨来趁鬼子不注意,一头扎到河里。鬼子向水里打枪,可是我们的雨来已经从水底游到远处去了。

鸡毛信

打竹板，台上站，
今天就来说抗战。
有个英雄叫海娃，
龙门村的儿童团。

这天他，边放羊，边放哨，
爸爸小跑到面前。
去，快把这信送王庄，
交给民兵张队长。
那是一封鸡毛信，
紧急情况写里边。

海娃赶羊去王庄，
不料碰到日本兵。
鸡毛信，哪里藏？
海娃抱起老绵羊，
把信绑在羊尾下。
鬼子抓住海娃搜，
搜来搜去没东西。

晚上到了小村庄。
鬼子宰羊烤羊肉，
吃饱喝足睡大觉。

海娃偷偷跑出来
取了信往山上跑。

谁知又把信丢了，
只好顺路往回找。
找到信，去王庄，
又被鬼子抓住了。
还让海娃来带路。

海娃把鬼子带进山，
四处山头枪声响。
原来是民兵张队长，
消灭了鬼子打胜仗。
海娃，海娃，小英雄，
鸡毛信的故事天下传。

资料

中国的抗日战争

中国抗日战争（1931—1945），或称日本侵(qīn)华战争，是日本侵略中国引起的战争，也是第二次世界大战东亚战事的主要部分。

抗日老照片

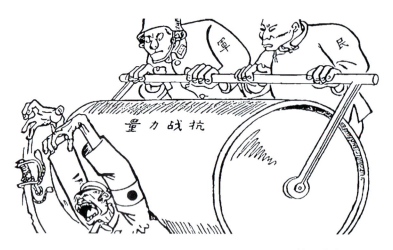

抗日战争时期漫画

Lesson seven

The Letter with Feathers

The story happened during the period of Anti-Japanese Invasion War. Haiwa was fourteen years old in that year. He was the leader of the Children's Group in Longmen Village. One day in the late afternoon, Haiwa was herding sheep on the mountain while on sentry duty when his father rushed to him, took out a letter and said, "Go to Wang Village at once and send the letter to Captain Zhang of the militia." Haiwa took the letter in hand and had a look at it. The letter was inserted with three chicken feathers, meaning it was very urgent. Haiwa put it away in a safe place and immediately drove the sheep onto the road.

Unluckily, on the foot of the hill, he saw a group of Japanese soldiers coming to rob staple food. The Japanese soldiers came nearer and nearer. Haiwa was very anxious. Where should he hide the letter with chicken feathers? Looking at the fat tail of the sheep, an idea came to his mind. He quickly held the old leader sheep and tied the letter to the underside of its tail. Haiwa stood up, threw the whip with a loud sound, and drove the sheep towards the Japanese soldiers.

"Stop!" Yelled the Japanese soldiers. With a "clatter", all the guns were raised and pointed at Haiwa's head. Haiwa was pulled to the Japanese officer. He deliberately tilted his head, opened his mouth wide, and looked at the officer foolishly. The soldiers searched Haiwa's entire body, even his two worn-out shoes, but found nothing. Still, they did not release Haiwa, but forced him to drive the sheep flock behind them.

The sun went down, the Japanese soldiers stopped in a small village. They slaughtered a few sheep and roasted the mutton to eat. Haiwa had no mind to feel bad about his sheep. He secretly put his hand under the old sheep's big tail and touched it. The letter was still there! He was relieved. After the Japanese soldiers ate their fill, they went to sleep with their guns in their arms and let Haiwa sleep in the innermost place. Haiwa could not sleep. He thought, "The Japanese soldiers will slaughter more sheep tomorrow. If I can't get away tonight, the letter with chicken feathers will be found." When all the soldiers were sound asleep, he gently stepped over the their thighs, ran out to the old sheep, held its tail and untied the letter, put it in his pocket, and ran to the mountain in one breath.

The sun rose up. Haiwa climbed onto the top of the mountain where he saw a Japanese soldier waving a small white flag back and forth towards him. Haiwa took off his white cloth and waved it back and forth the same way as the Japanese soldier. Unexpectedly he passed by. He ran to the top of the opposite hill and the Wang Village was not far away. Haiwa was very happy. He slumped down on the hill, his hand reached into his pocket and felt it, and then he began to shiver. Where is the chicken feather letter? There was nothing in his pocket! Haiwa searched all the cracks of the rocks around him, but there was nothing. Haiwa immediately ran back along the way, while running and looking. He ran to the place where he shook his clothes; the letter of chicken feathers was lying there. Haiwa was so happy. He put the letter in his pocket and just wanted to run back, but the Japanese soldiers came again. They grabbed and forced him to be their guide.

Haiwa walked in the front, driving the sheep flock. On a hill slope, he drove the sheep into a small sheep trail. The trail became harder and harder to walk, the Japanese soldiers walked on and off and lagged far behind. "Slow down!" the Japanese yelled at him. Haiwa took no notice of them and ran with all his might. The Japanese soldiers fired at him. Too exhausted to continue, Haiwa fell down to a pile of wild grasses. From the top of the hill suddenly rang out a burst of gunfire. Haiwa recognized it was the gunfire sound of his own people.

When Haiwa opened his eyes, he saw none other than Captain Zhang. He asked, "Letter-chicken feather letter?" Captain Zhang stroked Haiwa's head and said, "Don't worry. I received it. You brought the Japanese soldiers to the dead end and we wiped out the enemy. Thank you! You are a little hero!"

Yulai Was not Dead

Yulai was a 12 years old boy, who lived in the village of Reed Catkins. Along the village edge there was a river. In summer, Yulai would dive in and out of the river like fish together with his friends. Father said it was not OK if he didn't attend school, so he put Yulai in the night school. The textbook of Yulai was mimeographed on hand-made paper. Yulai put it on his lap and listened to the female teacher who taught all the students to learn the words. She read, "We are Chinese people. We love our mother land." All the students read after her in a soft voice.

The Japanese invaders began another round of "sweeping out". Father left home to fight against the Japanese invaders. One day, messenger Uncle Li ran into Yulai's home as the Japanese soldiers shouted loudly in the street. Uncle Li quickly moved the water tank in the corner and jumped down the hole under it, telling Yulai, "Yulai, move the tank back here and tell nobody about this." Yulai moved the water tank back to its original place. Barely did he come to the living room, the Japanese soldiers had rushed in. They asked Yulai, "Someone ran in here just now. Did you see him?" Yulai answered, "I was inside the room. I didn't see anything." The soldiers twisted his two ears, pulled his ears to both sides, and slapped him on his face. It hurt so much that Yulai saw stars in his eyes; his nose was bleeding. Tired of beating him, the Japanese yelled angrily, "Get him out and shoot him!" Folks of village of Reed Catkins heard several gun shots ring out by the river. They all cried.

After the Japanese devils left, people came to the river. Ah! A small head showed up on the water, picking at the reeds and asking, "The devils are gone?" "Yulai was not dead!" Everyone shouted happily. It turned out that before the gun went off, Yulai took advantage of the devils' inattention and dove headfirst into the river. The Japanese devils shot into the water, but our Yulai had already swum far away from the bottom of the river.

Information

China's War of Resistance against Japan

China's War of Resistance against Japan, or the War of Anti-Japanese Invasion (1931-1945), was a war fought between Japan and China after Japan invaded China. It's a major part of the East Asian War of World War II.

第八课

考 试

上课了,教语文的陈老师拿着考卷走进高一(4)班说:"开学两周了,今天进行一次考试。"又是突然考试,完了完了,死定了!有人叫着。但是卷子一到手,大家便埋头答题。陈老师出的卷子总是满满当当,不抓紧时间很难做完。

不过,半小时后,有些人开始活动了。余发首先想到的救兵是王笑天。他偷偷地看了老师一眼:老师望着窗外。余发放心了,将问题写在小纸条上,揉成一团扔给最后一排的王笑天。这时,老师转过身来,可是纸团不偏不倚正好落在后面的垃圾桶里。老师看了一眼,没有言语,低头改作业。余发连忙又扔了一个纸团过去。老师拿起来一看,是张白纸,说了句:"上课不要乱扔垃圾。"

刘艺 画

作弊虽然不成,但也没被老师抓着,余发暗自得意:"老师怎么斗得过学生!"不过余发不敢再作弊了。陈老师看起来在改作业,实际上是一心两用。传条子,翻书,偷看都不行,余发只能硬着头皮自己做了。

考卷一般是先易后难，但是余发找来找去，没一道题是容易的！看来只能撞大运了，撞好了，也许能及格呢。余发伸出左手，四个手指代表ABCD，心中一边默念儿歌，眼睛一边数着手指。儿歌一停，数到哪个手指，就把编号填在选择题上。

"老师，请多给一张纸。" 一位同学说。他叫陈明，头发有点儿乱，好像是没有梳头，但是很"Cool"。他是这个班的学霸，老师给了陈明纸，看了看他的卷子，满意地笑了。所有的人都抬起眼睛看着陈明，那目光有赞叹，有嫉妒：这家伙又要第一了！

这时欣然在想，《长江三日》的作者是谁？考前还看过这课，怎么给忘了呢？慌乱中欣然回头看看萧(xiāo)遥。他正在答题。考前谁都说"我没看书啊，我没背啊"，可真考起来，一个比一个答得快，答得多。

下课了，老师一边整理卷子，一边问欣然："上次考试，你成绩不如以前。怎么，好像有心事？"

"没——没有。"

"没有就好。女孩子大了，心容易散，不要放松。"

欣然想："我哪儿敢放松啊，恨不得一天32小时才好。"

同学们三三两两地离开教室。欣然站在路边，心想平时考试都很好，但是这回——难道是因为他？欣然倒吸了一口凉气。

这时，她看见王笑天、萧遥在打篮球，心一下子热了起来。

王笑天是校篮球队的主力队员，一个"小帅哥"，也是不少女生心中的"白马王子"。他球打得好，每次比赛，那漂亮的三步上篮，定能引起喝彩。每当这时，王笑天便向着球迷们，举举拳头，头发往后一甩，让球迷们兴奋。

不隐瞒地说，九中不少女生背后悄悄地给王笑天打过"100分"。可欣然认为男孩子光是英俊是不行的，还要有能力、有才气、性格好。她心中也有打"满分"的人，那就是班长萧遥。

才华和英俊的相貌相比，女孩子们更容易偏向才华。欣然觉得自己的那份情是淡淡的，浅浅的，但是并不轻松——这种感觉她是绝对不会对别人说的，何况也说不清楚。

欣然望着萧遥的背影，若有所思。

（根据郁秀著《花季雨季》选段改编）

生词

yú 余	Yu (surname)	shuài gē 帅哥	handsome boy
róu 揉	knead, roll	hè cǎi 喝彩	cheer
bù piān bù yǐ 不偏不倚	balanced	xīng fèn 兴奋	excited
zuò bì 作弊	cheat	yǐn mán 隐瞒	conceal, hide
zhuàng dà yùn 撞大运	luck	cái huá 才华	talent
jí gé 及格	pass the examination	yīng jùn 英俊	handsome
xuǎn zé 选择	choose	piān xiàng 偏向	deviate
shū tóu 梳头	comb one's hair	qiǎn 浅	subtle, shallow
xué bà 学霸	a student with excellent grades	jué duì 绝对	absolute
jí dù 嫉妒	jealousy	hè kuàng 何况	let alone
chéng jì 成绩	grade, achievement		

听写

揉　撞大运　及格　选择　梳头　成绩　帅哥

喝彩　兴奋　隐瞒　英俊　偏向　浅　绝对

何况　*余　不偏不倚　嫉妒

比一比

奋 { 兴奋 / 勤奋 }　　浅 { 水浅 / 浅蓝 }　　揉（揉纸）/ 柔（柔软）

隐　　　　　急
隐藏　　　　急忙

组词游戏

华

才华——华人——华侨——华夏——华商

华语广播——华文教育——中华民族

近义词

隐藏——隐瞒　　　英俊——帅

反义词

深——浅　　　　　隐瞒——公开

偏——正　　　　　英俊——丑陋

词语运用

虽然……但是……

① 虽然作弊不成，但是没被老师发现。

② 虽然她学习很好，但是身体太差。

③ 虽然山上的空气好，但是风很大。

硬着头皮

① 偷看不行，余发只好硬着头皮自己做考卷。

② 弟弟硬着头皮把苦药汤喝完了。

③ 晚上回家时，车灯突然坏了一个，我硬着头皮把车开回家。

词语解释

暗自得意——心里感到非常满意但不表现出来。

硬着头皮——勉强去做困难的或不愿意做的事情。

若有所思——好像在想什么。

赞叹——赞美感叹。

阅读

考试难

秦梦佳:Lindsay Qin(十年级)

试题似乎好几千,待做功课逾万篇。

停笔叹气不能答,偷偷四顾瞄一眼。

旁边同学护考卷,前面老师不走远。

从小次次考满分,现在作业做不完。

考试难,考试难,多选题,蒙着圈。

做完考题交老师,放学直奔奶茶店。

徐雨亭　画

写作练习

议论文中"举例子"说明道理

- 议论文是要求把道理讲清楚。
- 大段的论述往往不如举出合适的例子更能说明道理。
- 在举完例子之后,把道理总结出来。

范文

规　则

杨索菲(suǒ fēi)（九年级）

　　哎呀,快要晚了!飞机还有一个小时就要起飞了!可是姐姐已经在这个红灯前面等了好一会儿了。她要去纽约汇报工作,心急如火。她把空调开到了最大最冷,想冷静一下。她心想:"别的方向都已经轮到了,直行的直行,右转的右转,怎么就不给左转绿灯呢?不行,再这么等下去……"她左右看了看,周围一辆车都没有。于是她一点一点地往前蹭(cèng),穿过了第一条白线,她犹豫(yóu yù)了一下,违反交通规则值得吗?算了没时间了,就冲吧!她最后又往四周察看了一遍,没有车也没有警察(jǐng),一踩油门就往前冲。

　　刚过第二条白线,突然从旁边的小路上冒出了一辆警车。警车闪着鲜艳的警灯,快速地跟上了姐姐的车。看到警车时,姐姐的心里咯噔(gē dēng)了一下,完了!飞机赶不上还得被罚钱。停车之后,只见警察慢悠悠地走过来,皱(zhòu)着眉头说:"你现在看一看那个灯是什么颜色。要是你再等十秒钟,那个灯就会变绿。"姐姐把头转过去,看着变绿的交通灯,心里真是后悔呀!

　　生活给我们设的每一条规则我们都一定要遵(zūn)守,不是做给警察或别人看的,而是为了我们自己和他人的安全。我们就是自己生活中的警察。

Lesson Eight

Exam

The class began. Teacher Chen of language arts, walked into Class Four of 10th grade with examination papers in hand and said, "It's been two weeks since the beginning of the school year. We'll have an examination today." Another exam without notice. "I am done, I am done! I am Dead!" Some people screamed. But as soon as the paper was in hand, everyone buried their heads in answering the questions. Mr. Chen's papers were always full of questions. It was hard to finish them without hurrying.

However, after half an hour, some began to fuss about. The savior Yu Fa first thought of was Wang Xiaotian. Yu Fa secretly glanced at the teacher who was looking outside the window. Feeling at ease, Yu Fa wrote his problem in a slip of paper, rolled it into a small ball, and threw it at Wang Xiaotian who sat in the last row. Right at the moment, the teacher turned his body, and the paper ball fell right into the dustbin. The teacher looked at it. Without saying anything he began to correct the homework. Yu Fa hurried to throw another paper ball. The teacher picked it up and found it to be a piece of blank paper. He said, "Don't throw litter around in a class."

Although he was not able to cheat, he was not caught by the teacher. Yu Fa was secretly complacent, "How can the teacher outsmart the students!" But he did not dare to cheat again. Teacher Chen seemed to be correcting homework, but in fact he was multitasking. Passing notes, flipping through books and peeking at others were all impossible, so Yu Fa had to bite the bullet and did the test by himself.

The questions in the exam were usually easy first and then became hard, but Yu Fa looked around and didn't find a single easy question. It seemed that he could only rely on his luck. If he was lucky, he could pass. Yu Fa stretched out his left hand, using four fingers to represent ABCD. He silently recited a nursery rhyme, while his eyes counted the fingers. When the nursery rhyme stopped, he stopped at certain finger. Whichever letter the finger represented would be filled in the bracket of the multiple-choice questions.

"Teacher, please hand me another sheet of paper," said one student. His name was Chen Ming, whose hair is a little messy seemingly uncombed but quite cool. He was the top student in the class. The teacher handed him a sheet of paper, took a look at his exam paper, and smiled with satisfaction. All of the classmates raised their head and gazed at Chen Ming, that gaze mixed with admiration and jealousy: this guy is going to be number one again!

At this moment, Xinran was thinking who the author of *Three Days on the Yangtze River* was. "I had read this lesson before the exam. How did I forget it?" In a panic, Xinran looked back at Xiao Yao. He was busy answering the questions. Before the test, everyone said, "I did not review the lessons. I did not memorize." But when the test came, each one answered faster and more.

When the class ended, the teacher asked Xinran while sorting out the papers, "In the previous exam, your score was not as good as before. What's up? You have something on your mind?"

"No-nothing."

"If there is nothing, that's good. When a girl is older, her mind is easily distracted. Don't be too relaxed."

Xinran thought, "How dare I relax! I wish there were 32 hours a day."

The classmates left the classroom in small groups. Xinran stood on the side of the road, thinking, "I usually do well in exams. But this time-is it because of him?" Xinran gasped.

At that moment, she saw Wang Xiaotian and Xiao Yao playing basketball, and her heart warmed up at once.

Wang Xiaotian was the main player of the school basketball team, a "handsome guy", and also the "Prince Charming" for many girls. He played basketball very well. In every match, his beautiful three step layups were sure to draw applause. Whenever this happened, Wang Xiaotian would raise his fist towards the fans and flip his hair back, making the fans very excited.

It is not a secret that many girls in the Number Nine High School had quietly given Wang Xiaotian a score of 100 behind his back. But Xinran believed that boys needed to be not only handsome, but also capable, talented, and amicable. She also had someone in mind with a full score, and that one was the class president Xiao Yao.

Girls are more likely to favor talent compared to handsome looks. Xinran felt that her share of feeling was light and shallow, but not carefree. She would never tell others about this feeling, which was inexplainable anyway.

Xinran looked at Xiao Yao's back, lost in thought.

(Adapted from excerpts from *Seasons of Flower and Rain* by Yu Xiu)

Exams Are Hard

Qin Mengjia (Grade Ten)

There seem to be several thousands of exam questions. More than ten thousand homework await to be done.

I paused my pen and sighed, because I didn't know the answer. I looked around and wanted to peek at someone.

The classmates on my side guarded her exam papers. The teacher in the front wouldn't walk any farther.

I always had full scores in my exams when I was younger. But now I can't even finish my homework.

The exams are hard! Hard are the exams!

For multiple choice questions, I can only blindly guess.

After finishing the exam, I handed the paper to the teacher.

Straight to the milk tea shop I will go when school is over.

第九课

《卧虎藏龙》选段

一天,玉小姐正在房间里读书,忽听外面大厅传来父亲生气的声音。玉小姐见厅下跪着一个军官。父亲说:"养兵千日,用兵一时。一百骑兵也不算少,为何银子、武器被抢?"那军官道:"我们刚进沙漠,忽见远处起了一排黄云。有人大叫'不好,半天云来了!'话音刚落,马贼飞骑来到。我们马上迎战,可是领头的马贼十分勇猛,官兵遇到他,非死即伤。没多久,被他打死打伤的弟兄已有二十多个。听说他外号叫半天云,可他的姓名、年龄、相貌,都没人知道。有人说他少年英俊,也有人说他老当益壮……"

刘艺　画

第九课

　　第二天一早，玉帅亲自带兵出发捉马贼。玉帅走后，玉小姐带了两名卫兵，骑马到城外草原散心。她问卫兵："那马贼为何叫半天云？"卫兵说："他带着一帮人马，在沙漠中出没，冲过来时尘沙飞入天空，就像起了半天长云，因此得名。"又说："别看半天云是个马贼，专门和官家、草原上的头人作对，可草原上的人都护着他呢。"

　　进入草原，玉小姐的马像箭一样飞跑，没多久，就把两名卫兵甩在后面。忽然她听到马蹄声响，一看，有匹马赶了上来。马上的人二十来岁，短粗身材，浓眉毛，三角眼，衣着华丽，面带邪笑，说："哪里飞来的小鸟，真美呀！"玉小姐哪里受过这般轻薄，顺手就向那人一鞭挥去。那人躲过鞭子，伸手拉住玉小姐的腰带。二人一拉一扯，两匹马也慢慢停了下来。

　　玉小姐涨红了脸，喝道："你不想活了？"那人嬉皮笑脸地说："我还想活呢！告诉你，我是巴格，跟了我是你的福气！"巴格只顾用力将玉小姐往自己马上拉。正在这时，不远处一匹火红色的马冲过来，巴格躲闪不及跌下马来。玉小姐见马上的人，头戴一顶皮毛，遮住眉毛，身穿白布衫，身材壮实。那人用鞭子指着巴格喝道："光天化日之下，欺负一个弱女子，你算什么汉子！"

　　巴格说道："你是什么人？敢来管我巴格的事！"汉子说：

"我就是草原上专门打狼的人。巴格,我劝你少作恶!"巴格偷偷拔出腰上的短刀,猛地向那汉子刺去。玉小姐一旁看得明白,惊呼:"留神!"

那汉子十分敏捷,一把抓住巴格的手,用力一扭,只听巴格大叫一声,刀便落到地上。那汉子转过脸看着玉小姐,眼神里带着关切说:"看你不像草原上的人,这儿不是你玩儿的地方,还是回家吧。"

这时,后面的马蹄声又响了,三个人回头一看,玉小姐高兴地说:"我的人来了。"那汉子眼里突然闪出厌恶的目光。他说了句:"啊,原来你们都是一个庙里的神,我才多管闲事!"说完,向草原深处飞奔而去。"巴格赶快上马,只说了句:"原来你是军营中人,得罪!"也急忙跑了。玉小姐让卫兵去追巴格,卫兵说巴格是格桑头人的儿子,不好惹,还是算了吧。在回城的路上她想:"巴格不好惹,那汉子为何不把他放在眼里呢?他是什么样的人呢?"玉小姐好像还在梦里。

(根据王度庐原著《卧虎藏龙》及聂云岚改写本《玉娇龙》选段改编)

第九课

生词

wò 卧	crouch, lie	xī pí xiào liǎn 嬉皮笑脸	grin cheekily
mǎ zéi 马贼	thief, bandit	zhē zhù 遮住	cover
nián líng 年龄	age	bù shān 布衫	cloth shirt
xiàng mào 相貌	looks, appearance	guāng tiān huà rì 光天化日	daylight
lǎo dāng yì zhuàng 老当益壮	old but vigorous	qī fu 欺负	bully
sàn xīn 散心	relieve boredom	zuò è 作恶	do evil
xié 邪	evil	mǐn jié 敏捷	nimble
qīng bó 轻薄	flirt, slight	yàn wù 厌恶	detest
yāo 腰	waist	xián shì 闲事	other people's business
chě 扯	pull	rě 惹	provoke

听写

卧　马贼　年龄　邪　腰　扯　遮住　布衫

光天化日　欺负　作恶　敏捷　厌恶　闲事　惹

*轻薄　嬉皮笑脸

比一比

武 { 武器 / 武术 }　　　　负 { 欺负 / 负责 }

跌 { 跌倒 / 跌下 }　　　　厌 { 厌恶 / 讨厌 }

龄　　　　　　　令
年龄　　　　　　命令

组词游戏

闲

闲着——休闲——闲聊——闲静——闲散

忙里偷闲——说闲话——管闲事——闲不住

近义词

遮住——盖住　　　留神——小心　　　小偷——贼

相貌——面容　　　年岁——年龄　　　勇敢——勇猛

反义词

闲——忙　　　　　　欺负——爱护

厌恶——喜爱　　　　闲事——正事

多音字

恶 è　作恶

巴格，我劝你少作恶！

恶 wù　厌恶

他眼里闪出厌恶的目光。

喝 hē { 喝水 / 喝酒 }

喝 hè { 喝道 / 喝彩 }

词语运用

欺负

① 哥哥爱帮助人，从不欺负人。

② 在游乐场里，有人不排队，还欺负别人。

③ 妹妹在学校从不欺负别人，但也不受别人欺负。

敏捷

① 击剑运动员的动作十分敏捷。

② 他动作敏捷，几下就爬上了一棵大树。

③ 华华知识丰富，思想敏捷，学习成绩优秀。

词语解释

非死即伤——不是死就是受伤。

留神——小心。

关切——关心。

得罪——使人不快或怀恨。

思考题

1. 官兵的银子、武器被谁抢了？

2. 为什么草原上的人护着半天云？

3. 带皮帽子的汉子救了玉小姐，他是谁？

第九课

资料

武侠小说简介

金庸

武侠小说，是中国文学中的大众文学。早在唐朝就已出现。自民国以后风行于华人地区，是一种结合历史与幻(huàn)想(xíng)的小说类型。武侠小说多以中国古代历史为背景，小说人物的价值观是行侠仗(zhí)义。著名的新派武侠小说家有金庸(yōng)、古龙及梁羽生等。他们把历史、爱情、神魔、武侠四者结合起来，故事曲折(zhé)，人物鲜活，娱(yú)乐性强且富有传统文化内涵(hán)。

侠客

Lesson Nine

Excerpted from *Crouching Tiger, Hidden Dragon*

One day, when Lady Jade was reading a book inside her room she heard from the outside hall the angry voice of her father. She peeked and saw an officer kneel down in the hall. Her father scolded, "Train the army for a thousand days to combat for one battle. A cavalry of one hundred soldiers is not small. Why did the silver and weapons get robbed?" The officer said, "We had just entered the desert when we suddenly saw a row of yellow clouds in the distance. Someone shouted, 'No good! The Half-sky Cloud is coming!' The words just fell and the horse thieves came on flying horses. We immediately fought against them, but the leader of the horse bandits was very brave. Whoever encountered him was either killed or wounded. In a short time, he killed and wounded more than 20 brothers. I heard that his nickname was Half-sky Cloud, but his name, age, appearance, no one knew. Some say he is young and handsome; some say he is old but strong…"

The next morning, leading the troops himself, Marshal Jade set out to catch the horse thieves. After he left, Lady Jade took two guards and rode to the grassland outside the city to take a break. She asked the guards, "Why is that horse thief called Half-sky Cloud?" The guards said, "He led a group of people and horses haunting the desert. When they rushed over, the dust and sand flew into the sky like clouds covering half the sky, hence the name." And they also said, "Although Half-sky Cloud is a horse thief, especially rebelling against the officials and the tribe leader of the grassland, people of the grassland are all protecting him."

Entering the grassland, Lady Jade's horse flew like an arrow, and left the two guards far behind in no time. Suddenly she heard the sound of hoofbeats. She looked back and saw a horse rush up. The man on the horse was about twenty years old, short and thick, with thick eyebrows and triangular eyes and gorgeously dressed. With an evil smile on his face, he said, "Where did you little bird fly from? You are really beautiful!" Having never suffered such a slight, Lady Jade immediately swung her whip to that person. The man dodged the whip, reached out and pulled Lady Jade's belt. The two pulled and tugged; the two horses also slowly stopped.

Lady Jade turned red and rebuked him, "You don't want to live?" The man said boisterously, "I still want to live! I'm telling you: I'm Bugger. It will be your fortune to be my woman." Bugger only cared about pulling Lady Jade towards his horse. At that moment, from not afar, a fiery red horse rushed over. Bugger didn't have time to dodge and fell off the horse. Lady Jade looked at the man on the horse, who wore a fur cap covering his eyebrows, in a white cloth shirt, looking very strong. The man pointed his whip at Bugger and shouted, "Bully a weak woman under bright daylight! What kind of a man are you!"

Bugger said, "Who are you? How dare you come to meddle in my Bugger's business!" The man said, "I am the man who specializes in fighting wolves on the grassland. Bugger, I advise you to do less evil!" Secretly pulling out the short knife on his waist, Bugger stabbed at the man violently. Clearly seeing Bugger's action from the side, Lady Jade exclaimed in alarm, "Be careful!"

The man was very agile. With one hand he grabbed Bugger's hand and gave it a strong twist. Bugger shouted loudly and the knife fell to the ground. The man turned his face and looked at Lady Jade. With concern in his eyes, he said, "I see you are not one from the grasslands. This is not a place for you to play in. You'd better go home."

At this time, the sound of hooves beat behind again. The three of them turned back to look. Lady Jade said happily, "My people are coming." The man's eyes suddenly flashed with disgust. He said, "Ah, so you are all gods in one temple. I just meddled!" Having said that, he galloped away into the grassland. Bugger quickly mounted his horse and simply said, "So you are from the military camp, excuse me!" He also hurriedly rode away. Lady Jade asked the guards to chase Bugger but was told Bugger was the son of the head of the Gesang who was not to be messed with. She had to let it go. On the way back to the town she thought, " If Bugger is not to be messed with, why did that young man treat him with contempt? What kind of person is he?" Lady Jade seemed to be still in the dream.

(Adapted from the original *Crouching Tiger, Hidden Dragon* by Wang Dulu and the rewriting version of *Yu Jiaolong/Jade Delicate Dragon* by Nie Yunlan)

Brief Introduction to Martial Arts Novels

The Martial Arts novel is a popular genre in Chinese literature. Having been around since the Tang Dynasty and becoming very popular since the Republic of China in Chinese communities, it is a genre of fiction that combines history and fantasy. Most martial arts novels are set in the ancient Chinese history background, and the values of the characters are about chivalry and justice. Famous new Martial Arts novelists include Jin Yong, Gu Long, and Liang Yusheng. They combined history, romance, spiritual magic, and martial arts in stories which, with twists and turns, and with its vivid characters, are both entertaining and rich in traditional cultural connotations.

第十课

宝玉和黛玉

那日黛玉下船上了轿子,到了荣国府。几个穿红着绿的丫头笑迎上来说:"林姑娘来了!"

黛玉一进房,见两个人扶着一位银发老太太迎上来。黛玉知是外祖母,正要下拜,早被外祖母搂入怀中,"心肝儿肉"叫着大哭起来,黛玉也哭个不停。这时,听到后院有笑声说:"我来迟了!"只见丫头们拥着一个丽人进来。这人身材苗条,衣着彩绣,美若仙子,一双丹凤三角眼,两弯柳叶吊梢(shāo)眉。姐妹们说:"这是琏(liǎn)嫂子。"黛玉虽不识,也曾听母亲说过,这是大舅之子

中国人民邮政《红楼梦》邮票(1981年)

贾琏的妻子，叫王熙(xī)凤。这熙凤拉着黛玉的手，上下细细打量笑道："天下真有这样漂亮人儿！我今日才算看见了。"又问："妹妹几岁了？可上过学？现吃什么药？在这里别想家，要什么吃的、什么玩的，只管告诉我。"黛玉一一答应。

吃过茶，黛玉去见王夫人。王夫人说："你三个姐妹都好，以后一处念书认字，学针线。我只一件事不放心，我有个'混世魔王'，今日去庙里还没回来。你以后不用理他，这些姐姐妹妹都不敢沾惹他的。"黛玉曾经听母亲说过，她的表兄含玉而生，不喜读书，外祖母又溺爱，无人敢管。黛玉笑道："舅母所说，可是含玉而生的？在家时母亲常说，这位哥哥比我大一岁，小名叫宝玉，性虽顽皮，但与姐妹们极好。"王夫人笑道："你哪里知道，他小时和姐妹们相处惯了，若姐妹们不理他倒还好，要是哪天姐妹们和他多说了一句话，他心上一喜，便生出许多事来。"黛玉一一的都答应着。

贾母问黛玉念何书。黛玉道："刚念了《四书》。"正说着，只听外面一阵脚步响，有人说："宝玉来了。"进来一看，却是位青年公子：头戴宝石紫金冠，身穿百蝶大红上衣，面若中秋之月，色如春晓之花，眉如墨画，睛若秋波，脖子上挂着一块美玉。黛玉一见便大吃一惊，心想："好奇怪，倒像在哪里见过的，何等眼熟！"

贾母笑道："还不去见你妹妹呢。"宝玉早看见了一个秀丽的女儿，料定是林姑妈之女，忙来见礼。细看时，真是与众各别。只见：两弯似蹙(cù)非蹙笼烟眉，一双似喜非喜含情目；泪光点点，娇喘微微；闲静似娇花照水，行动如弱柳扶风。宝玉看罢，笑道："这个妹妹我曾见过的。"贾母笑道："又胡说了，你何曾见过？"宝玉笑道："虽没见过，却看着面善，心里倒像是远别重逢的一般。"贾母笑道："好！这就和睦了。"

宝玉走向黛玉身边坐下，问："妹妹可曾读书？"黛玉道："不曾读书，只上了一年学，认得几个字。"宝玉又问黛玉："可有玉没有？"黛玉答道："我没有玉。你那玉是件宝物，哪能人人都有？"宝玉听了，突然摘下那玉狠命摔去，骂道："什么宝物！人的高下不识，我也不要了！"贾母急得搂了宝玉道："你生气要打骂人容易，不能摔那命根子！"宝玉哭道："家里姐妹都没有，单我有；如今来了个天仙似的妹妹也没有，可知这不是个好东西。"贾母忙哄他道："你这妹妹原有玉来着。你姑妈去世时，将玉带走了。"说着从丫头手中接过玉来给他带上。宝玉听了，信以为真，也就不再说什么了。

（根据曹雪芹著《红楼梦》第三回改编）

生词

dài yù 黛玉	Daiyu (name)	zhān 沾	touch
jiào zi 轿子	sedan chair	céng jīng 曾经	once, formerly
yā tou 丫头	wench, maid	nì ài 溺爱	love blindly, spoil
fú zhe 扶着	hold	wán pí 顽皮	naughty
lǒu 搂	embrace	guān 冠	headgear, hat
xiù 绣	embroidery	bó zi 脖子	neck
sǎo 嫂	sister-in-law	xián jìng 闲静	quiet, tranquil
jiù 舅	uncle	bà 罢	finish
jiǎ 贾	Jia (surname)	chóng féng 重逢	reunion
dǎ liang 打量	look at	hé mù 和睦	harmony
mó wáng 魔王	prince of the devils	hǒng 哄	coax

听写

轿子　扶着　搂　绣　嫂　舅舅　贾　打量　沾

曾经　顽皮　冠　脖子　罢　和睦　*溺爱

重逢　哄

比一比

料 { 料定 / 不料 / 材料 }

轿 { 轿子 / 轿车 }

溺
溺爱

弱
弱小

组词游戏

料

不料——料定——材料——布料

饮料——绸料——难料——学习材料

近义词

抱——搂　　顽皮——调皮　　狠命——拼命

反义词

闲——忙　　　　不肯——同意

料定——不料　　和睦——争斗

多音字

liáng
量
测量

liàng
量
大量

词语运用

曾经

① 我曾经读过《红楼梦》这本书,很喜欢。

② 我们家曾经在德国住过五年。

③ 这里曾经是一片松树林,现在已经成了公园了。

和睦

① 邻居们相处十分和睦,从来没有吵过架。

② 哥哥在家对弟弟妹妹非常友爱,家里很和睦。

词语解释

料定——料想一定是这样。

下拜——指跪下行礼。

衣着——身上的穿戴，服装的式样，穿戴的方式。

苗条——身材细长柔美。

丹凤眼——眼睛细长，细而不小，眼尾微上翘。

表兄——舅、姨、姑的儿子，年长自己的叫表兄。

写作练习

读《红楼梦》中人物的描写：

> 身材苗条，衣着彩绣，美若仙子。
> 一双丹凤三角眼，两弯柳叶吊梢眉。

> 头戴宝石紫金冠，身穿百蝶大红上衣。
> 面若中秋之月，色如春晓之花，眉如墨画，睛若秋波。

> 两弯似蹙非蹙笼烟眉，一双似喜非喜含情目。
> 闲静似娇花照水，行动如弱柳扶风。

描写一个人物：

从身材、衣着、面容、动作等方面细致描写

第十课

资料

作者简介

《红楼梦》原名《石头记》，是中国古代优秀的长篇小说之一。作者曹雪qín芹（约1715—约1764），清朝人。

《红楼梦》一书共描写了400多个人物，作品语言优美而有诗意，再现了当时生活场景和细节。全书以贾宝玉、林黛玉、薛宝钗（xuē chāi）的爱情悲剧为中心主线，描写了贾家这个封建贵族大家庭衰（shuāi）亡的过程。宝玉反对男尊女卑、追求平等和个性解放；黛玉重爱情，轻功名，她和宝玉的爱情与这个封建家庭产生了矛盾。本课描写了黛玉初到外祖母家，第一次见到宝玉的情景。

本文人物

贾宝玉：贾母的孙子，王夫人的儿子。

林黛玉：贾母的外孙女，宝玉的表妹。

王熙凤：贾琏的妻子，宝玉的嫂子。

贾母：宝玉的奶奶，黛玉的姥姥。

王夫人：宝玉的母亲，黛玉的舅妈。

电视连续剧《红楼梦》剧照：贾宝玉

电视连续剧《红楼梦》剧照：薛宝钗

电视连续剧《红楼梦》剧照：林黛玉

Lesson Ten

Baoyu and Daiyu

On that day, Daiyu disembarked from the ship and got on a sedan chair and arrived at Rongguo Mansion. Several maids wearing bright clothing came up with smiles and said, "Lady Lin has arrived!"

The instant Daiyu entered the room, she saw a silk-haired old lady helped by two servants walk towards her. Knowing she was her grandmother, Daiyu was going to kneel down, but was held in arms by her grandmother who called "my beloved" and cried out loud. Daiyu began to cry too. At this moment, she heard someone speaking with laughter from the back yard, "I am late!" In came a beautiful lady waited upon by many maids. With a slim figure, wearing beautiful embroidered clothes, the lady was as beautiful as a fairy, having the almond-shaped eyes of a phoenix, slanting eyebrows as long and drooping as willow leaves. The cousins told her, "This is our sister-in-law, wife of second brother Lian." Lady Xifeng held Daiyu's hands, looked at her carefully up and down, and said with smiles, "There is such great beauty in this world! Today I finally get to see!" Then she continued to ask, "Little sister, how old are you? Have you been to school? What medicine do you take now? Don't miss home in this place. Whatever you want to eat or play with, just tell me." Daiyu answered all the questions one by one.

After drinking tea, Daiyu went to meet Madam Wang. Madam Wang said to her, "Your three sisters are all very good. You will be together to study and do needlework. I have only one worry: I have a "chaos-creating devil", who went to the monastery and hasn't come back yet. Don't pay any attention to him. None of your cousins dares to provoke him." Daiyu heard from her mother that her cousin brother was born with a piece of jade inside his mouth who didn't like studying, had been spoilt by grandmother, and nobody dared to discipline him. Daiyu smiled and said, "Is Aunty talking about my cousin who was born with a piece of jade in his mouth? When I was at home my mother often talked with me about him. I know from her this cousin is a year older than I am. His nickname is Baoyu and although he is a little naughty, he is very nice to the sisters." Madam Wang smiled and said, "You have no way to know. He is used to growing up with his sisters. He is OK if the sisters pay no attention to him; if on any day any sister talks with him for one more sentence, which makes him happy, he will surely create a lot of trouble. " Daiyu promised her to follow her advice.

Grandmother asked Daiyu what books she had studie. Daiyu answered, "I just finished the *Four Books*." While they were talking, she heard footsteps from the outside. Someone said, "Baoyu is coming." She saw a young man come in who wore a purple gold crown with precious stones and a bright red top embroidered with a hundred butterflies. His face was like the full moon of mid-autumn, as pretty as a flower in a spring morning. His eyebrows were dark as if drawn by ink, his

eyes like wave in autumn, and in his neck hang a piece of jade. The instant Daiyu saw him she was very surprised and thought to herself, "How strange! I feel so familiar with him as if I have met him before."

Grandma laughed and said, "Hurry and meet your younger sister." Baoyu had already seen a beautiful young girl, knowing she must be the daughter of his aunt, quickly came to greet her. He looked carefully at her and found her so unique with her arch eyebrows which seemed to be half knitting, a pair of eyes full of emotion half joyous. There seemed to be teardrops in her eyes; when she breathed, one could almost hear the faint panting. She was still like a flower in the riverside; when she moved, her slender body was like the weak willow waving with the wind. Baoyu finished checking on her and began to laugh and said, "I have seen this younger sister before." Grandma laughed and said, "You are talking nonsense again. When did you ever see her?" Baoyu smiled and answered, "Although we haven't met before, but I see she has a very kind face, and I feel as if we are reuniting after being apart for a long time." Grandma laughed and said, "Wonderful! Then you two will enjoy harmony!"

Walking towards Daiyu and sitting beside her, Baoyu asked, "Has my younger sister studied any books?" Daiyu answered, "I haven't studied any books. I only attended school for one year and learned a few characters." Baoyu continued to ask Daiyu, "Do you have a jade?" Daiyu answered, "I don't have a jade. Your jade is a unique treasure. How can everyone have it?" Hearing this, Baoyu suddenly took off his jade and threw it to the ground with all his might. He cursed, "What kind of treasure! It doesn't know the good and bad among people. I don't want it anymore!" Grandma anxiously hugged Baoyu and said, "You can hit or scold people as you please if you are angry. But you cannot throw your lifeline!" Baoyu cried, "None of the sisters in the family has a jade, but only I do. Now such a goddess like sister comes and still doesn't have a jade. Apparently, this is not a good thing." Grandma hurried to coax him, saying, "This sister of yours used to have a jade. When your aunt passed away, the jade accompanied her." With such words she took the jade from the maids and put it back on him. Believing she told the truth, Baoyu stopped saying anything else.

(Adapted from Chapter Three of *Dream of the Red Chamber* by Cao Xueqin)

Brief Introduction of the Author

Dream of the Red Chamber, originally entitled *The Story of the Stone*, is one of the excellent novels in ancient China. Its author is Cao Xueqin (c. 1715—1764), who lived in Qing Dynasty.

Dream of the Red Chamber depicts vividly more than 400 characters in beautiful and poetic language, recreating the scenes and details of life at that time. Using the love tragedy among Jia Baoyu, Lin Daiyu, and Xue Baochai as the central story line, the book portrays the decline of the Jia family, a large feudal aristocratic family. Baoyu opposes the superiority of men over women and pursues equality and individual liberation; Daiyu values love over fame. Their love conflicts with the feudal family. This lesson describes the happenings when Daiyu came to her grandma's home and met Baoyu for the first time.

The characters in this text are Jia Baoyu, the grandson of Grandma Jia and the son of Madam Wang. Lin Daiyu: the daughter of Grandma Jia's daughter, Baoyu's cousin. Wang Xifeng: Jia Lian's wife, Baoyu's sister-in-law. Mother Jia: Baoyu's paternal grandmother, Daiyu's maternal grandmother. Lady Wang: Baoyu's mother, Daiyu's aunt.

生字表（简）

1. 冈(gāng) 继(jì) 续(xù) 晕(yūn) 吼(hǒu) 竖(shù) 趁(chèn) 尽(jìn) 截(jié) 锤(chuí) 劲(jìn) 赤(chì)
   恐(kǒng)

2. 扭(niǔ) 擦(cā) 胭(yān) 脂(zhī) 谈(tán) 戴(dài) 缠(chán)

3. 诸(zhū) 葛(gě) 瑜(yú) 刁(diāo) 缺(quē) 负(fù) 责(zé) 督(dū) 鲁(lǔ) 舱(cāng)

4. 私(sī) 吩(fēn) 咐(fù) 靠(kào) 寨(zhài) 鼓(gǔ) 悉(xī) 仍(réng) 散(sàn) 丞(chéng)

5. 悟(wù) 僧(sēng) 摘(zhāi) 戒(jiè) 菩(pú) 萨(sà) 份(fèn) 棒(bàng) 拦(lán) 随(suí) 尸(shī) 箍(gū) 咒(zhòu)
   毫(háo) 拨(bō) 呆(dāi)

6. 陋(lòu) 铭(míng) 斯(sī) 苔(tái) 痕(hén) 帘(lián) 鸿(hóng) 儒(rú) 牍(dú) 庐(lú) 蜀(shǔ)

7. 抗(kàng) 哨(shào) 搜(sōu) 哆(duō) 嗦(suō)

8. 揉(róu) 偏(piān) 倚(yǐ) 弊(bì) 择(zé) 梳(shū) 霸(bà) 嫉(jí) 绩(jì) 帅(shuài) 奋(fèn) 隐(yǐn) 瞒(mán)
   俊(jùn) 浅(qiǎn) 况(kuàng)

9. 卧(wò) 贼(zéi) 龄(líng) 益(yì) 邪(xié) 腰(yāo) 扯(chě) 嬉(xī) 遮(zhē) 衫(shān) 欺(qī) 恶(è) 敏(mǐn)
   捷(jié) 厌(yàn) 闲(xián) 惹(rě)

10. 黛(dài) 轿(jiào) 丫(yā) 扶(fú) 搂(lǒu) 绣(xiù) 嫂(sǎo) 舅(jiù) 贾(jiǎ) 沾(zhān) 溺(nì) 曾(céng)
　　脖(bó) 冠(guān) 罢(bà) 逢(féng) 睦(mù) 哄(hǒng)

共计 123 个生字

生字表（繁）

1. 岡(gāng) 繼(jì) 續(xù) 暈(yūn) 吼(hǒu) 豎(shù) 趁(chèn) 盡(jìn) 截(jié) 錘(chuí) 勁(jìn) 赤(chì)
   恐(kǒng)

2. 扭(niǔ) 擦(cā) 胭(yān) 脂(zhī) 談(tán) 戴(dài) 纏(chán)

3. 諸(zhū) 葛(gě) 瑜(yú) 刁(diāo) 缺(quē) 負(fù) 責(zé) 督(dū) 魯(lǔ) 艙(cāng)

4. 私(sī) 吩(fēn) 咐(fù) 靠(kào) 寨(zhài) 鼓(gǔ) 悉(xī) 仍(réng) 散(sàn) 丞(chéng)

5. 悟(wù) 僧(sēng) 摘(zhāi) 戒(jiè) 菩(pú) 薩(sà) 份(fèn) 棒(bàng) 攔(lán) 隨(suí) 屍(shī) 箍(gū) 咒(zhòu)
   毫(háo) 撥(bō) 呆(dāi)

6. 陋(lòu) 銘(míng) 斯(sī) 苔(tái) 痕(hén) 簾(lián) 鴻(hóng) 儒(rú) 牘(dú) 廬(lú) 蜀(shǔ)

7. 抗(kàng) 哨(shào) 搜(sōu) 哆(duō) 嗦(suō)

8. 揉(róu) 偏(piān) 倚(yǐ) 弊(bì) 擇(zé) 梳(shū) 霸(bà) 嫉(jí) 績(jì) 帥(shuài) 奮(fèn) 隱(yǐn) 瞞(mán)
   俊(jùn) 淺(qiǎn) 況(kuàng)

9. 臥(wò) 賊(zéi) 齡(líng) 益(yì) 邪(xié) 腰(yāo) 扯(chě) 嬉(xī) 遮(zhē) 衫(shān) 欺(qī) 惡(è) 敏(mǐn)
   捷(jié) 厭(yàn) 閒(xián) 惹(rě)

10. 黛(dài) 轎(jiào) 丫(yā) 扶(fú) 摟(lǒu) 綉(xiù) 嫂(sǎo) 舅(jiù) 賈(jiǎ) 沾(zhān) 溺(nì) 曾(céng)
   脖(bó) 冠(guān) 罷(bà) 逢(féng) 睦(mù) 哄(hǒng)

共計 123 個生字

生词表（简）

1. 梁山 酒店 冈 劝告 布告 继续 晕 扑 吼 竖
   趁着 用尽 两截 正好 铁锤 使劲 赤手空拳
   争先恐后 赏钱

2. 经商 招呼 身材 扭捏 擦 胭脂 稀奇古怪 别扭
   首饰 化妆品 谈 不由分说 戴 扎 缠 浑身

3. 诸葛亮 才智 周瑜 刁难 缺少 负责 推辞 都督
   花费 恐怕 误事 签 鲁肃 探听 蒙 安放 船舱
   秘密

4. 私自 调用 动静 吩咐 划 靠近 水寨 敲鼓 熟悉
   埋伏 迎战 好像 插满 仍旧 散去 大功告成
   丞相 神机妙算

5. 悟 僧 摘 戒 妖精 运气 菩萨 徒弟 埋怨
   不知好歹 份 棒子 拦住 随便 假尸 紧箍咒 毫毛
   挑拨 呆子 筋斗

6. 陋室 铭 斯吾 苔痕 帘 鸿儒 案牍 庐 蜀

7. 抗日战争 儿童 放哨 紧急 绵羊 绑 鞭 搜
村庄 心疼 混 哆嗦 拼命 消灭

8. 余 揉 不偏不倚 作弊 撞大运 及格 选择 梳头
学霸 嫉妒 成绩 帅哥 喝彩 兴奋 隐瞒 才华
英俊 偏向 浅 绝对 何况

9. 卧 马贼 年龄 相貌 老当益壮 散心 邪 轻薄
腰 扯 嬉皮笑脸 遮住 布衫 光天化日 欺负 作恶
敏捷 厌恶 闲事 惹

10. 黛玉 轿子 丫头 扶着 搂 绣 嫂 舅 贾 打量
魔王 沾 曾经 溺爱 顽皮 冠 脖子 闲静 罢
重逢 和睦 哄

共计 178 个生词

生词表（繁）

1. 梁山 酒店 岡 勸告 佈告 繼續 暈 撲 吼 豎
   趁着 用盡 兩截 正好 鐵錘 使勁 赤手空拳
   爭先恐後 賞錢

2. 經商 招呼 身材 扭捏 擦 胭脂 稀奇古怪 別扭
   首飾 化妝品 談 不由分說 戴 紮 纏 渾身

3. 諸葛亮 才智 周瑜 刁難 缺少 負責 推辭 都督
   花費 恐怕 誤事 簽 魯肅 探聽 蒙 安放 船艙
   秘密

4. 私自 調用 動靜 吩咐 劃 靠近 水寨 敲鼓 熟悉
   埋伏 迎戰 好像 插滿 仍舊 散去 大功告成
   丞相 神機妙算

5. 悟 僧 摘 戒 妖精 運氣 菩薩 徒弟 埋怨
   不知好歹 份 棒子 攔住 隨便 假屍 緊箍咒 毫毛
   挑撥 呆子 筋斗

6. 陋室(lòu shì) 銘(míng) 斯(sī) 吾(wú) 苔痕(tái hén) 簾(lián) 鴻儒(hóng rú) 案牘(àn dú) 廬(lú) 蜀(shǔ)

7. 抗日戰爭(kàng rì zhàn zhēng) 兒童(ér tóng) 放哨(fàng shào) 緊急(jǐn jí) 綿羊(mián yáng) 綁(bǎng) 鞭(biān) 搜(sōu) 村莊(cūn zhuāng) 心疼(xīn téng) 混(hùn) 哆嗦(duō suo) 拼命(pīn mìng) 消滅(xiāo miè)

8. 餘(yú) 揉(róu) 不偏不倚(bù piān bù yǐ) 作弊(zuò bì) 撞大運(zhuàng dà yùn) 及格(jí gé) 選擇(xuǎn zé) 梳頭(shū tóu) 學霸(xué bà) 嫉妒(jí dù) 成績(chéng jì) 帥哥(shuài gē) 喝彩(hè cǎi) 興奮(xīng fèn) 隱瞞(yǐn mán) 才華(cái huá) 英俊(yīng jùn) 偏向(piān xiàng) 淺(qiǎn) 絕對(jué duì) 何況(hè kuàng)

9. 卧(wò) 馬賊(mǎ zéi) 年齡(nián líng) 相貌(xiàng mào) 老當益壯(lǎo dāng yì zhuàng) 散心(sàn xīn) 邪(xié) 輕薄(qīng bó) 腰(yāo) 扯(chě) 嬉皮笑臉(xī pí xiào liǎn) 遮住(zhē zhù) 布衫(bù shān) 光天化日(guāng tiān huà rì) 欺負(qī fu) 作惡(zuò è) 敏捷(mǐn jié) 厭惡(yàn wù) 閑事(xián shì) 惹(rě)

10. 黛玉(dài yù) 轎子(jiào zi) 丫頭(yā tou) 扶着(fú zhe) 摟(lǒu) 繡(xiù) 嫂(sǎo) 舅(jiù) 賈(jiǎ) 打量(dǎ liang) 魔王(mó wáng) 沾(zhān) 曾經(céng jīng) 溺愛(nì ài) 頑皮(wán pí) 冠(guān) 脖子(bó zi) 閑靜(xián jìng) 罷(bà) 重逢(chóng féng) 和睦(hé mù) 哄(hǒng)

共計 178 個生詞

新双双中文教材 12

New Chinese Language and Culture Course

中国文学欣赏 Appreciation of Chinese Literature

练习本 单课

（第二版）

[美]王双双 编著

北京大学出版社
PEKING UNIVERSITY PRESS

目　录

第一课　　武松打虎 …………………………………… 1

第三课　　草船借箭（上）……………………………… 7

第五课　　孙悟空三打白骨精 ………………………… 13

第七课　　鸡毛信 ……………………………………… 18

第九课　　《卧虎藏龙》选段 ………………………… 23

第一课 武松打虎

一 写生词

冈					
晕					
扑					
吼					
竖					
梁	山				
酒	店				
劝	告				
布	告				
继	续				
趁	着				

用	尽				
两	截				
正	好				
铁	锤				
使	劲				
赏	钱				
赤	手	空	拳		
争	先	恐	后		

二 每字组二词

欣赏　趁早　布告　肯定

赏 { ☐

肯 { ☐

第一课
武松打虎

趁 { ☐   告 { ☐

三 下列汉字是由哪些部分组成的

晕 → ☐ + ☐   肯 → ☐ + ☐

四 选字组词

头（军 晕）　（锤 睡）觉　容（易 踢）

（军 晕）人　（锤 睡）子　（易 踢）球

五 给下面的词语加拼音

传开 _____　　　水浒传 _____

六 写出反义词

不肯—_____　　　竖—_____

第一课 武松打虎

七 将方框中的词语与适当的解释连线

赤手空拳	有很大的酒量。
争先恐后	没有任何武器，空手打斗。
敬重	争着向前，生怕落后。
喝酒海量	恭敬尊重。

八 选择填空

1. 店家说："这种酒叫'三碗不过冈'，是说人喝了三_____之后就会醉倒。"（杯 瓶 碗）

2. 武松说："我喝酒是海量，从来没_____。"（晕过 醉过）

3. 武松不听劝告，提着一根_____就上山去了。（绳子 棍子）

4. 老虎气得大_____一声。（吼 孔）

5. 武松想："我有棍子，怕什么虎！"就_____往前走。

   （继续 停止）

6. 爸爸_____古典音乐，我更喜欢摇滚乐。（欣赏 赏钱）

7. 每个周六，弟弟都去_____足球。（踢 易）

第一课 武松打虎

九 根据课文判断对错

1. 武松是一位梁山好汉，打虎英雄。　　　　　___对___错

2. 武松看到官府的布告才知道真的有老虎。　　___对___错

3. 武松喝多了酒，倒在一块空地上睡着了。　　___对___错

4. 武松用棍子打死了老虎。　　　　　　　　　___对___错

5. 武松的拳头像铁锤，很有劲。　　　　　　　___对___错

6. 武松把赏钱买酒喝了。　　　　　　　　　　___对___错

7. "武松打虎"是小说《水浒传》中的故事。　___对___错

十 造句

趁着_____

不肯_____

继续_____

十一 写作练习

给句子加上合适的词语让句子生动

哈哈　哗啦哗啦地　声音像打雷一样　嘴角微微一笑

第一课 武松打虎

- 例：大雨下了一整天。

  大雨哗啦哗啦地下了一整天。

- 武松大笑着说："我喝酒是海量。"

  _____

- 老虎大吼一声。

  _____

- 他考试得了100分，拿着考卷满意地走了。

  _____

十二 缩写课文《武松打虎》（不少于8句话，加标点）

第一课 武松打虎

十三 选词填空

- 人们去理发的店叫＿＿＿＿＿＿。
- 卖日用品的店叫＿＿＿＿＿＿。
- 可以吃饭的店叫＿＿＿＿＿＿。
- 卖书的店叫＿＿＿＿＿＿。
- 人们外出可以住宿和吃饭的地方叫＿＿＿＿＿＿。
- 卖衣服的商店叫＿＿＿＿＿＿。

书店　旅店　饭店　理发店　服装店　百货商店

十四 熟读课文两遍，讲"武松打虎"的故事（连续表达2分钟）

第三课
草船借箭（上）

一 写生词

签					
蒙					
才	智				
周	瑜				
刁	难				
缺	少				
负	责				
推	辞				
都	督				
花	费				

恐	怕				
误	事				
鲁	肃				
探	听				
安	放				
船	舱				
秘	密				
诸	葛	亮			

二 组新字

知 + 日 → ☐　　　舌 + 辛 → ☐

叔 + 目 → ☐　　　舟 + 仓 → ☐

鱼 + 日 → ☐　　　禾 + 必 → ☐

第三课 草船借箭（上）

三 每字组二词

探险　花钱　秘书　安放

花 { _____
　　 _____

探 { _____
　　 _____

安 { _____
　　 _____

秘 { _____
　　 _____

四 选字组词

（误　吴）事　　　（秘　必）密　　　（愿　原）来

姓（误　吴）　　　（秘　必）须　　　（愿　原）意

五 给下面的词语加拼音

必须 _____　　　　秘密 _____

六 写出反义词

推辞—_____　　　　刁难—_____

秘密—_____　　　　借钱—_____

第三课
草船借箭（上）

七 将方框中的词语与适当的解释连线

自有妙用	完不成任务，自愿受死的保证书。
板起脸	自然有巧妙的用处。
生死文书	话说得过分，超过实际才能。
说大话	不高兴，脸上没有笑容。
军中无戏言	军队中讨论作战时，不可以开玩笑。

八 选词填空

1. 诸葛亮才智过人，周瑜对他一直_____。

2. 周瑜让诸葛亮十天造十万支箭_____诸葛亮。

3. 诸葛亮对周瑜说_____十天造箭，恐怕会误事。

4. 周瑜派鲁肃去诸葛亮那里_____情况。

5. 周瑜说："是他自己送死，不是我_____的。"

九 根据课文判断对错

1. 周瑜才智过人，诸葛亮总是刁难他。　　　　　____对____错

第三课
草船借箭（上）

2. 水陆交战，只有周瑜认为弓箭最好。　　____对____错

3. 诸葛亮答应三天交出十万支箭。　　____对____错

4. 鲁肃是周瑜的手下，也是诸葛亮的好朋友。　　____对____错

5. 诸葛亮让鲁肃背着周瑜帮他的忙。　　____对____错

十　给带点的字加拼音

1. 周瑜总是刁难（　　　　）诸葛亮。

2. 他唱歌有些难（　　　　）听。

十一　造句

恐怕_____

花费_____

十二　周瑜是怎样刁难诸葛亮的？写出他们的对话（加标点）

周　瑜：_____

_____

第三课
草船借箭（上）

诸葛亮：_____

周　瑜：_____

_____

诸葛亮：_____

周　瑜：_____

_____

诸葛亮：_____

周　瑜：_____

_____

诸葛亮：_____

周　瑜：_____

_____

诸葛亮：_____

第三课 草船借箭（上）

十三 创意写作

帮诸葛亮写一份"生死文书"给周瑜

生死文书

_____
_____
_____
_____
_____
_____
_____

签字_____

日期_____

十四 熟读课文两遍

第五课
孙悟空三打白骨精

一 写生词

悟						拦	住				
僧						随	便				
摘						假	尸				
戒						毫	毛				
份						挑	拨				
妖	精					呆	子				
运	气					筋	斗				
菩	萨					紧	箍	咒			
徒	弟										
埋	怨					不	知	好	歹		
棒	子										

二 每字组二词

随 { ⎯⎯⎯⎯⎯⎯ }   戒 { ⎯⎯⎯⎯⎯⎯ }

怨 { ⎯⎯⎯⎯⎯⎯ }   摘 { ⎯⎯⎯⎯⎯⎯ }

第五课
孙悟空三打白骨精

三 选字组词

活（泼　拨）　　（摘　滴）花　　随（便　更）

挑（泼　拨）　　（摘　滴）水　　（便　更）好

四 给下面的词语加拼音

头发 _____　　活泼 _____　　挑拨 _____

五 写出反义词

举起—_____　　　　松—_____

暗自高兴—_____

六 将方框中的词语与适当的解释连线

胡言乱语	没有根据地瞎说。
暗自高兴	不能辨别好坏，指人糊涂。
二话不说	心里高兴但不表现出来。
不知好歹	不说话，很干脆地采取行动。
一干二净	形容一点儿也不剩。

第五课 孙悟空三打白骨精

七 选词填空

1. 悟空让八戒沙僧保护师父,就_____桃林而去。

2. 唐僧忙上前拦住说:"不要_____伤人!"

3. 悟空疼得在地上打滚,妖精看见_____。

4. 唐僧的大_____是孙悟空。

5. 孙悟空一个_____回到了花果山。

八 根据课文判断对错

1. 唐僧师徒四人去西天取经。　　　　　　　　　____对____错

2. 妖精听说吃了唐僧肉能长生不老。　　　　　　____对____错

3. 唐僧、八戒、沙僧都没认出白骨精。　　　　　____对____错

4. 猪八戒总是跟师父说孙悟空的好话。　　　　　____对____错

5. 孙悟空不怕妖精,就怕师父念紧箍咒。　　　　____对____错

6. 唐僧听了八戒的挑拨,把悟空赶走了。　　　　____对____错

7. 孙悟空三打白骨精都是为了保护师父。　　　　____对____错

第五课
孙悟空三打白骨精

九 给带点的字加拼音

1. 八戒说:"饭三个人不吃,等猴子回来就得(　　　)四个人分。"

2. 圣诞节我们都得(　　　)到了很多礼物。

十 回答问题

1. 西游记的作者是谁? _____

2. 唐僧师徒四人是哪四人? _____

3. 孙悟空有哪些本领? _____

4. 猪八戒有哪些缺点? _____

十一 造句

随便_____

埋怨_____

第五课
孙悟空三打白骨精

十二 创意写作

题目：让我做一回孙悟空

十三 熟读课文两遍，讲讲"孙悟空三打白骨精"的故事（连续表达1~2分钟）

第七课 鸡毛信

一 写生词

绑					
鞭					
搜					
混					
儿	童				
放	哨				
紧	急				
绵	羊				

村	庄				
心	疼				
哆	嗦				
拼	命				
消	灭				
抗	日	战	争		

二 组新字

占 + 戈 → ☐   立 + 里 → ☐

日 + 免 → ☐   代 + 衣 → ☐

米 + 曹 → ☐   一 + 火 → ☐

第七课 鸡毛信

赶紧　消息　动脑　拼音

三　每字组二词

脑 { _____ _____ }　　　拼 { _____ _____ }

紧 { _____ _____ }　　　消 { _____ _____ }

四　选字组词

（傍　旁）晚　　　吃（饱　包）　　　（绵　棉）羊

（傍　旁）边　　　钱（饱　包）　　　（绵　棉）花

五　给下面的词语加拼音

傍晚 _____　　　　　旁边 _____

六　写出反义词

战争—_____　　　　　儿童—_____

绑上—_____　　　　　饱—_____

第七课 鸡毛信

七 将方框里的词句与适当的解释连线

儿童团　　　　十分爱惜，珍惜。

心疼　　　　　儿童的抗日组织，负责放哨送信等。

羊道　　　　　羊和牧人走的路，很难走。

八 选词填空

1. 海娃在山上一边放羊，一边_____。

2. 信上插着三根鸡毛，是一封很_____的信。

3. 日本兵_____几只羊烤羊肉吃。

4. 海娃把羊赶上了一条_____。

5. 日本兵吼道："慢慢的！"海娃不理他，_____往前跑。

九 根据课文判断对错

1. 故事发生在抗日战争时期。　　　　____对____错

2. 海娃十四岁，是龙门村儿童团的团长。　　　　____对____错

3. 海娃把鸡毛信藏在老绵羊的尾巴下面。　　　　____对____错

第七课
鸡毛信

☆------------☆------------☆

4. 海娃把鸡毛信丢了,后来一直没有找到那封信。　　___对___错

5. 海娃把日本兵带上了一条羊道。　　___对___错

十　给带点的字加拼音

1. 秋天满地都是落（　　　）叶。

2. 海娃赶着羊走在前面,日本兵远远落（　　　）在后面。

十一　造句

拼命_____

糟糕_____

十二　阅读作业

根据阅读课文《雨来没有死》选词填空

1. 雨来喜欢游泳,在_____钻上钻下。（河里　海里）

2. 爸爸叫雨来上了_____。（中学　夜校）

3. 雨来把书放在_____。（腿上　书桌上）

4. 女老师教大家_____。（认字　唱歌）

第七课
鸡毛信

5. 李大叔跑进雨来家,把_____的缸搬开。(墙角　墙上)

6. 雨来_____鬼子不注意,一头扎到河里。(赶　趁)

十三　选做题:了解一下中国的抗日战争

提示:中国抗日战争是第二次世界大战的一部分。发生的时间、地点、何时结束?

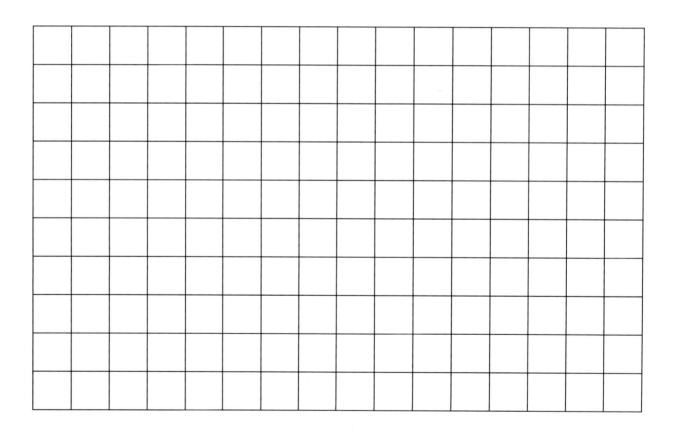

十四　熟读课文

第九课
《卧虎藏龙》选段

一 写生词

卧					
邪					
腰					
扯					
惹					
马	贼				
年	龄				
相	貌				
散	心				
轻	薄				
遮	住				
布	衫				

欺	负				
作	恶				
敏	捷				
厌	恶				
闲	事				
老	当	益	壮		
嬉	皮	笑	脸		
光	天	化	日		

二 组新字

女 + 喜 → ☐　　　若 + 心 → ☐

臣 + 卜 → ☐　　　月 + 要 → ☐

门 + 木 → ☐　　　每 + 文 → ☐

第九课 《卧虎藏龙》选段

三 选字组词

年（龄　令）　　拉（扯　止）　　（敏　每）捷

命（龄　令）　　停（扯　止）　　（敏　每）天

四 每字组二词

闲话　跌下　武术　负责

武 {　　　　　}　　　　负 {　　　　　}

闲 {　　　　　}　　　　跌 {　　　　　}

五 给下面的词语加拼音

年龄　_____　　　命令　_____

六 写出反义词

闲—_____　　　　欺负—_____

厌恶—_____　　　闲事—_____

第九课 《卧虎藏龙》选段

七 找出近义词，连线

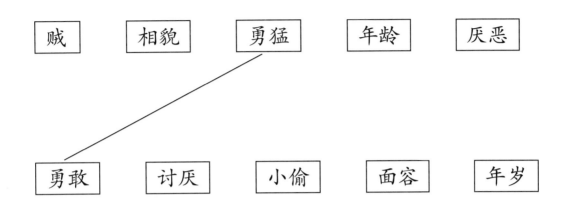

八 将方框中的词语与适当的解释连线

老当益壮	使人不愉快或怀恨。
光天化日	大家看得非常清楚的场合。
留神	年纪虽老而志气更旺盛，干劲更足。
得罪	小心。
嬉皮笑脸	嬉笑不严肃或轻浮的样子。

九 选词填空

1. 马贼外号半天云，他的姓名、年龄、_____都没人知道。

2. 玉小姐带了卫兵，骑马到城外草原_____。

3. 巴格_____地说："我还想活呢！"

第九课
《卧虎藏龙》选段

☆------------☆------------☆

4. 汉子说:"原来你们都是一个庙里的神,我才多管_____!"

5. 巴格说了句:"原来你是军营中人,_____!"

6. 别看妹妹_____小,在台上唱歌可大方了。

7. 叔叔学过武术,现在五十多岁了,动作还是那么_____。

十 根据课文判断对错

1. 领头的马贼外号叫半天云。 ___对___错

2. 半天云很厉害,官兵遇到他,非死即伤。 ___对___错

3. 马贼专门和官家、草原上的头人作对。 ___对___错

4. 巴格想欺负玉小姐。 ___对___错

5. 有个汉子救了玉小姐。 ___对___错

6. 玉小姐是王帅的女儿。 ___对___错

7. 玉小姐想知道救他的汉子是谁。 ___对___错

十一 给带点的字加拼音

1. 那汉子说:"巴格,我劝你少作恶(_____)。

第九课 《卧虎藏龙》选段

2. 他眼睛里闪出了厌恶（　　　）的目光。

3. 天气太热，爸爸进屋就喝（　　　）水。

4. 玉小姐对巴格喝（　　　）道："你不想活了？"

十二 造句

欺负＿＿＿＿＿＿＿＿＿＿＿＿＿＿＿＿＿＿＿＿＿＿＿＿

十三 创意写作

题目"玉小姐日记一篇"

提示词：马贼　半天云　散心　巴格　欺负　汉子　汉子是谁

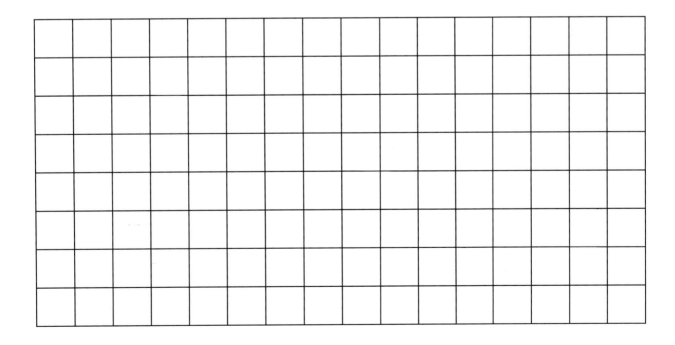

十四 熟读课文，讲一讲"卧虎藏龙"的故事（连续表达1~2分钟）

第一课　听写

1.	2.	3.	4.
5.	6.	7.	8.
9.	10.	11.	12.

第三课　听写

1.	2.	3.	4.
5.	6.	7.	8.
9.	10.	11.	12.

第五课　听写

1.	2.	3.	4.
5.	6.	7.	8.
9.	10.	11.	12.

第七课　听写

1.	2.	3.	4.
5.	6.	7.	8.
9.	10.	11.	12.

第九课 听写

1.	2.	3.	4.
5.	6.	7.	8.
9.	10.	11.	12.

1.	2.	3.	4.
5.	6.	7.	8.
9.	10.	11.	12.

1.	2.	3.	4.
5.	6.	7.	8.
9.	10.	11.	12.

1.	2.	3.	4.
5.	6.	7.	8.
9.	10.	11.	12.

新双双中文教材 12
New Chinese Language and Culture Course

中国文学欣赏 Appreciation of Chinese Literature

练习本 单课

（第二版）

［美］王双双 编著

北京大学出版社
PEKING UNIVERSITY PRESS

目　录

第一课　武松打虎 …………………………………… 1

第三课　草船借箭（上） …………………………… 7

第五课　孙悟空三打白骨精 ………………………… 13

第七课　鸡毛信 ……………………………………… 18

第九课　《卧虎藏龙》选段 ………………………… 23

第一课 武松打虎

一 写生词

冈					
晕					
扑					
吼					
竖					
梁	山				
酒	店				
劝	告				
布	告				
继	续				
趁	着				

用	尽				
两	截				
正	好				
铁	锤				
使	劲				
赏	钱				
赤	手	空	拳		
争	先	恐	后		

二 每字组二词

欣赏　趁早　布告　肯定

赏 { _____

肯 { _____

第一课 武松打虎

趁 { _____　　　告 { _____

三 下列汉字是由哪些部分组成的

晕 → □ + □　　　肯 → □ + □

四 选字组词

头（军　晕）　　（锤　睡）觉　　容（易　踢）

（军　晕）人　　（锤　睡）子　　（易　踢）球

五 给下面的词语加拼音

传开 _____　　　水浒传 _____

六 写出反义词

不肯—_____　　　竖—_____

第一课
武松打虎

七 将方框中的词语与适当的解释连线

赤手空拳	有很大的酒量。
争先恐后	没有任何武器，空手打斗。
敬重	争着向前，生怕落后。
喝酒海量	恭敬尊重。

八 选择填空

1. 店家说："这种酒叫'三碗不过冈'，是说人喝了三_____之后就会醉倒。"（杯　瓶　碗）

2. 武松说："我喝酒是海量，从来没_____。"（晕过　醉过）

3. 武松不听劝告，提着一根_____就上山去了。（绳子　棍子）

4. 老虎气得大_____一声。（吼　孔）

5. 武松想："我有棍子，怕什么虎！"就_____往前走。

   （继续　停止）

6. 爸爸_____古典音乐，我更喜欢摇滚乐。（欣赏　赏钱）

7. 每个周六，弟弟都去_____足球。（踢　易）

第一课
武松打虎

九 根据课文判断对错

1. 武松是一位梁山好汉，打虎英雄。　　　　___对___错

2. 武松看到官府的布告才知道真的有老虎。　___对___错

3. 武松喝多了酒，倒在一块空地上睡着了。　___对___错

4. 武松用棍子打死了老虎。　　　　　　　　___对___错

5. 武松的拳头像铁锤，很有劲。　　　　　　___对___错

6. 武松把赏钱买酒喝了。　　　　　　　　　___对___错

7. "武松打虎"是小说《水浒传》中的故事。　___对___错

十 造句

趁着_____

不肯_____

继续_____

十一 写作练习

给句子加上合适的词语让句子生动

哈哈　哗啦哗啦地　声音像打雷一样　嘴角微微一笑

第一课
武松打虎

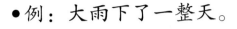

- 例：大雨下了一整天。

  大雨哗啦哗啦地下了一整天。

- 武松大笑着说："我喝酒是海量。"

  _____

- 老虎大吼一声。

  _____

- 他考试得了100分，拿着考卷满意地走了。

  _____

十二　缩写课文《武松打虎》（不少于8句话，加标点）

第一课
武松打虎

十三　选词填空

- 人们去理发的店叫＿＿＿＿＿＿＿＿。
- 卖日用品的店叫＿＿＿＿＿＿＿＿。
- 可以吃饭的店叫＿＿＿＿＿＿＿＿。
- 卖书的店叫＿＿＿＿＿＿＿＿。
- 人们外出可以住宿和吃饭的地方叫＿＿＿＿＿＿＿＿。
- 卖衣服的商店叫＿＿＿＿＿＿＿＿。

书店
旅店
饭店
理发店
服装店
百货商店

十四　熟读课文两遍，讲"武松打虎"的故事（连续表达2分钟）

第四课 草船借箭（下）

三 每字组二词

山寨　散场　埋了　派去

派 { _____
　 { _____

寨 { _____
　 { _____

散 { _____
　 { _____

埋 { _____
　 { _____

四 选字组词

（敲　高）鼓　　水（寨　赛）　　（派　旅）兵

（敲　高）楼　　比（寨　赛）　　（派　旅）行

五 给下面的字词加拼音

扔东西 _____　　仍旧 _____　　奶 _____

六 写出反义词

敌人—_____　　　　神机妙算—_____

第四课 草船借箭(下)

七 将方框中的词语与适当的解释连线

轻易　　　　　　朝着敌人来的方向上前去作战。

迎战　　　　　　取得很大的成功。

调用　　　　　　简单、容易；随随便便。

大功告成　　　　调动使用。

八 回答问题

小说《三国演义》的作者是_____。

九 选择填空

1. 诸葛亮向鲁肃借船，鲁肃_____派了二十条快船。

2. 诸葛亮的船队靠近了曹操的_____。

3. 诸葛亮让士兵一边_____，一边大喊。

4. 曹操_____一万多个弓箭手来到江边，一齐放箭。

5. 只过了一会儿，船上的稻草人身上就_____箭。

第四课
草船借箭（下）

十 根据课文判断对错

1. 一连两天，诸葛亮都没有动静。　　　　　　　　＿＿对＿＿错

2. 诸葛亮的船往江北划，这时江上下雨了。　　　　＿＿对＿＿错

3. 诸葛亮下令士兵敲鼓大喊。　　　　　　　　　　＿＿对＿＿错

4. 鲁肃怕曹军冲出来。　　　　　　　　　　　　　＿＿对＿＿错

5. 诸葛亮船上的稻草人身上插满了箭。　　　　　　＿＿对＿＿错

6. 草船借箭大功告成，诸葛亮得到十万多支箭。　　＿＿对＿＿错

7. 周瑜说："诸葛亮神机妙算，我比他强。"　　　　＿＿对＿＿错

十一 给带点的字加拼音

1. 我小的时候，最喜欢和同学一起去划船。（　　　）

2. 去欧洲旅行之前，我们做了详细的计划。（　　　）

十二 造句

派＿＿＿＿＿＿＿＿＿＿＿＿＿＿＿＿＿＿＿＿＿＿＿＿＿＿＿＿＿＿

第四课
草船借箭（下）

十三 创意写作

题目：如果你能和诸葛亮/周瑜见面，你想问什么问题？你有什么建议？

提示：问诸葛亮怎么知道哪天有雾。他懂得天文地理吗？

为什么不论天冷天热总拿把羽毛扇？

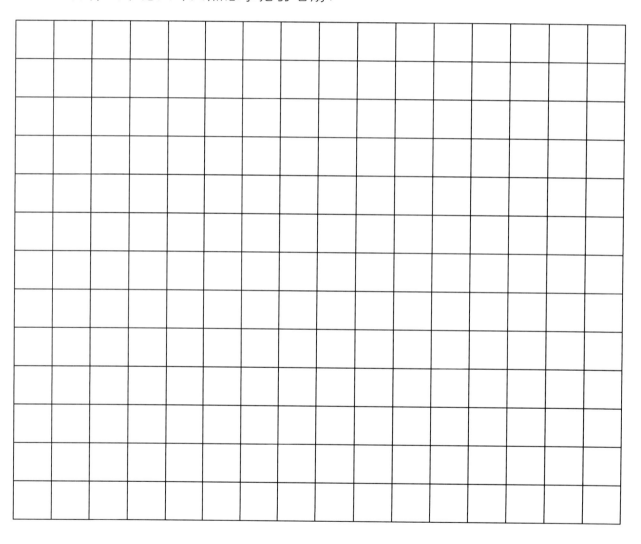

十四 熟读课文，讲一讲"草船借箭"的故事（连续表达1~2分钟）

第六课 陋室铭

一 写生词

铭					
斯					
吾					
帘					
庐					

蜀					
陋	室				
苔	痕				
鸿	儒				
案	牍				

二 下列汉字是由哪些部分组成的

吾 → □ + □

庐 → □ + □

诸 → □ + □

牍 → □ + □

三 每字组二词

海苔　丑陋　温馨　窗帘

陋 { _____ / _____ }

馨 { _____ / _____ }

苔 { _____ / _____ }

帘 { _____ / _____ }

第六课 陋室铭

四 选字组词

鸿（儒 需）　　青（苔 苔）　　案（读 牍）

必（儒 需）　　舞（台 苔）　　阅（读 牍）

五 给下面的字词加拼音

苔痕 _____　　　　吾 _____

温馨 _____　　　　新 _____

读书 _____　　　　案牍 _____

六 写出反义词

简陋—_____　　　　鸿儒—_____

第六课
陋室铭

七 将方框中的词语与适当的解释连线

德馨	博学多闻的儒者。
鸿儒	简陋的房屋。
陋室	不学无术的人。
白丁	品德高尚美好。
素琴	指官府的文书。
案牍	不加雕饰的琴。

八 根据《陋室铭》把句子补齐

1. 山不在高，有仙则名。＿＿＿＿＿＿，有龙则灵。

2. 斯是陋室，＿＿＿＿＿＿。

3. ＿＿＿＿＿＿，草色入帘青。

4. 谈笑有鸿儒，＿＿＿＿＿＿。

5. 可以调素琴，＿＿＿＿＿＿。

6. ＿＿＿＿＿＿，无案牍之劳形。

7. 孔子云："＿＿＿＿＿＿？"

第六课 陋室铭

九 根据课文判断对错

1. 山不在于高低，只要有神仙就是名山。　　　　＿＿对＿＿错

2. 水不在于深浅，只要有鱼虾便能显灵。　　　　＿＿对＿＿错

3. 房子虽然简陋，但这里人品好，好事多。　　　　＿＿对＿＿错

4. 来往的好友是饱学之士，也有不学无术之人。　　＿＿对＿＿错

5. 这儿可以弹钢琴，可以读经典。　　　　　　　　＿＿对＿＿错

6. 陋室远离闹市，更无公文劳身。　　　　　　　　＿＿对＿＿错

7. 孔子说过："这哪里是简陋呢？"　　　　　　　　＿＿对＿＿错

十 书法练习：将右边书法作品（繁体）抄写一遍，尽量写得像

山不在高有僊則名水不在深有龍則靈斯是陋室惟吾德馨

第六课
陋室铭

十一 抄写《陋室铭》(包括作者、标点)

十二 创作：试着按《陋室铭》形式填写新内容，写几句也行

　　提示：乒乓球、画画、唱歌、跳舞、打游戏、旅游等

十三 背诵课文《陋室铭》

第八课 考试

一 写生词

余					
揉					
浅					
作	弊				
及	格				
选	择				
梳	头				
学	霸				
嫉	妒				
成	绩				
帅	哥				

喝	彩				
兴	奋				
隐	瞒				
才	华				
英	俊				
偏	向				
绝	对				
何	况				
撞	大	运			
不	偏	不	倚		

二 组新字

化 + 十 ⟶ ☐　　　木 + 各 ⟶ ☐

大 + 田 ⟶ ☐　　　女 + 疾 ⟶ ☐

又 + 寸 ⟶ ☐　　　女 + 户 ⟶ ☐

第八课 考试

英雄　何时　华人　偏向

三 每字组二词

华 { _____
　　 _____

英 { _____
　　 _____

何 { _____
　　 _____

偏 { _____
　　 _____

四 选字组词

（隐　急）瞒　　（柔　揉）面　　（梳　流）头

（隐　急）忙　　温（柔　揉）　　（梳　流）水

五 给下面的词语加拼音

隐瞒 _____　　着急 _____

六 写出反义词

隐瞒—_____　　深—_____

英俊—_____　　偏—_____

第八课 考 试

七 将方框中的词语与适当的解释连线

暗自得意	勉强去做困难的或不愿意做的事情。
硬着头皮	心里感到非常满意但不表现出来。
若有所思	好像在想什么。

八 选词填空

1. 陈老师出的卷子总是_____。

2. 纸团_____正好落在后面的垃圾桶里。

3. 余发考试答不出题，只好_____了。

4. 陈平的卷子老师很满意，他是班里的_____。

5. 欣然觉得，男孩子光是_____是不行的。

6. 才华和相貌相比，女孩子更容易_____才华。

九 根据课文判断对错

1. 陈老师是高一（4）班的语文老师。 ____对____错

2. 余发考试想作弊，他的救兵是萧遥。 ____对____错

3. 考试时余发最后只好自己做题。 ____对____错

第八课 考 试

☆ ---------- ☆ ---------- ☆

4. 陈明学习好,是班里的学霸。　　　　　　　　____对____错

5. 王笑天篮球打得好,是个"小帅哥"。　　　　　____对____错

6. 萧遥是班长,欣然心里给他100分。　　　　　　____对____错

十　造句

虽然……但……_____

十一　根据课文回答问题

提示：作弊、篮球队的主力队员、小帅哥、男孩子光是英俊不行

1. 余发的学习好不好？课文中是怎样描写他的？

_____

_____

2. 许多女生心目中的"白马王子"是谁？只因为他会打篮球吗？

_____

_____

3. 欣然认为男孩子重要的是有才华、性格好。你的观点呢？

_____

第八课 考试

十二 写作

举例说明什么是"责任"/"规则"/"助人"

（三个题目选一题，250字）

范文

责 任

金 玫（八年级）

我十岁的时候，家里养了一只小仓鼠。它叫Alvin，只有D电池那么大。它虽然小却很活泼，每天晚上都会在仓鼠轮里面跑步。它可爱死了！我的责任是喂它食物和水，跟它玩儿，和妈妈一起清理笼子。

刚开始的时候，我担心它会长得太胖，于是只喂它建议的食量，没有再喂它额外的食物。圣诞节那几天，我们常不在家，去了很多聚会，我就忘记了喂Alvin。直到有一天，妈妈发现它四脚朝天躺在笼子里，我这才想起很长时间没有喂过它了，它被饿死了！我很难过，因为我的过失，一条小生命没有了。

从这次过失中，我学到了什么是责任：就是必须精心去做事，不能有半点儿马虎。现在我又养了一只小白兔，我保证对它负责，每天晚上都喂它。

第八课
考 试

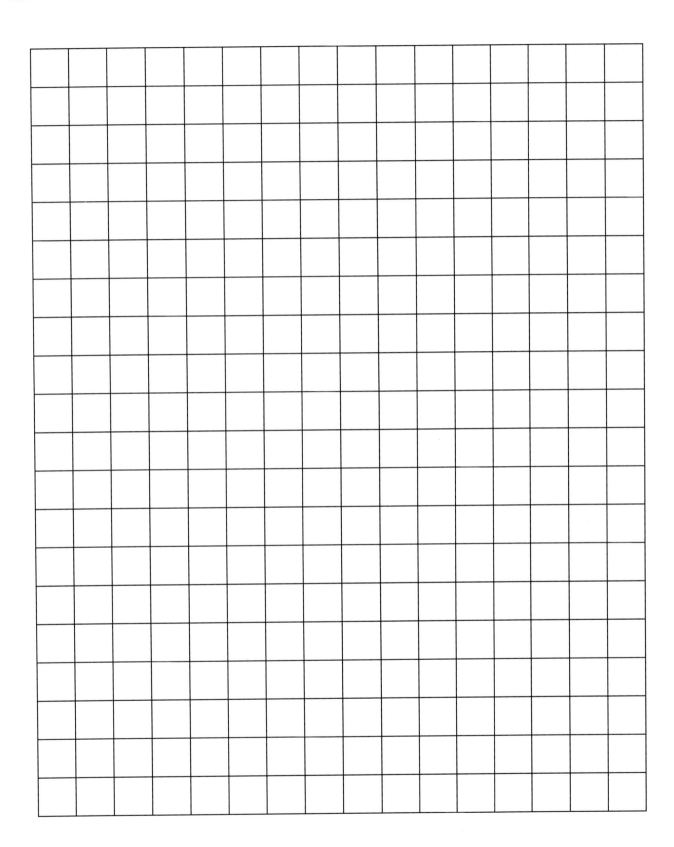

十三 熟读课文两遍

第十课 宝玉和黛玉

一 写生词

搂						丫	头				
绣						扶	着				
嫂						打	量				
舅						魔	王				
贾						曾	经				
沾						溺	爱				
冠						顽	皮				
罢						脖	子				
哄						闲	静				
黛	玉					重	逢				
轿	子					和	睦				

二 组新字

西 + 贝 ⟶ ☐   车 + 乔 ⟶ ☐

元 + 页 ⟶ ☐   口 + 共 ⟶ ☐

第九课
《卧虎藏龙》选段

一 写生词

卧					
邪					
腰					
扯					
惹					
马	贼				
年	龄				
相	貌				
散	心				
轻	薄				
遮	住				
布	衫				

欺	负				
作	恶				
敏	捷				
厌	恶				
闲	事				
老	当	益	壮		
嬉	皮	笑	脸		
光	天	化	日		

二 组新字

女 + 喜 → ☐　　　若 + 心 → ☐

臣 + 卜 → ☐　　　月 + 要 → ☐

门 + 木 → ☐　　　每 + 文 → ☐

第九课 《卧虎藏龙》选段

三 选字组词

年（龄 令）　　拉（扯 止）　　（敏 每）捷

命（龄 令）　　停（扯 止）　　（敏 每）天

四 每字组二词

闲话　跌下　武术　负责

武 { _____ / _____ }　　　负 { _____ / _____ }

闲 { _____ / _____ }　　　跌 { _____ / _____ }

五 给下面的词语加拼音

年龄 _____　　　命令 _____

六 写出反义词

闲—_____　　　欺负—_____

厌恶—_____　　　闲事—_____

第九课 《卧虎藏龙》选段

七 找出近义词，连线

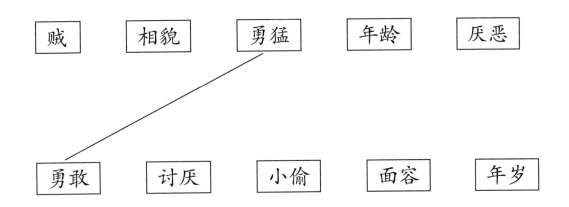

八 将方框中的词语与适当的解释连线

老当益壮	使人不愉快或怀恨。
光天化日	大家看得非常清楚的场合。
留神	年纪虽老而志气更旺盛，干劲更足。
得罪	小心。
嬉皮笑脸	嬉笑不严肃或轻浮的样子。

九 选词填空

1. 马贼外号半天云，他的姓名、年龄、_____都没人知道。

2. 玉小姐带了卫兵，骑马到城外草原_____。

3. 巴格_____地说："我还想活呢！"

第九课
《卧虎藏龙》选段

4. 汉子说:"原来你们都是一个庙里的神,我才多管_____!"

5. 巴格说了句:"原来你是军营中人,_____!"

6. 别看妹妹_____小,在台上唱歌可大方了。

7. 叔叔学过武术,现在五十多岁了,动作还是那么_____。

十 根据课文判断对错

1. 领头的马贼外号叫半天云。　　　　　　　　　___对___错

2. 半天云很厉害,官兵遇到他,非死即伤。　　　___对___错

3. 马贼专门和官家、草原上的头人作对。　　　　___对___错

4. 巴格想欺负玉小姐。　　　　　　　　　　　　___对___错

5. 有个汉子救了玉小姐。　　　　　　　　　　　___对___错

6. 玉小姐是王帅的女儿。　　　　　　　　　　　___对___错

7. 玉小姐想知道救他的汉子是谁。　　　　　　　___对___错

十一 给带点的字加拼音

1. 那汉子说:"巴格,我劝你少作恶(　　　)。

第九课 《卧虎藏龙》选段

2. 他眼睛里闪出了厌恶（　　　）的目光。

3. 天气太热，爸爸进屋就喝（　　　）水。

4. 玉小姐对巴格喝（　　　）道："你不想活了？"

十二　造句

欺负＿＿＿＿＿＿＿＿＿＿＿＿＿＿＿＿＿＿＿＿＿＿＿＿

十三　创意写作

题目"玉小姐日记一篇"

提示词：马贼　半天云　散心　巴格　欺负　汉子　汉子是谁

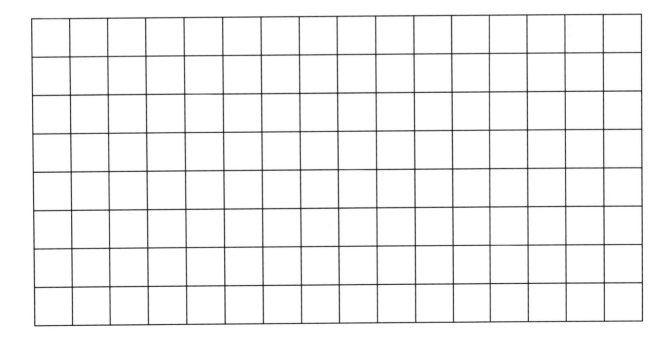

十四　熟读课文，讲一讲"卧虎藏龙"的故事（连续表达1~2分钟）

第一课　听写

1.	2.	3.	4.
5.	6.	7.	8.
9.	10.	11.	12.

第三课　听写

1.	2.	3.	4.
5.	6.	7.	8.
9.	10.	11.	12.

第五课　听写

1.	2.	3.	4.
5.	6.	7.	8.
9.	10.	11.	12.

第七课　听写

1.	2.	3.	4.
5.	6.	7.	8.
9.	10.	11.	12.

第九课　听写

1.	2.	3.	4.
5.	6.	7.	8.
9.	10.	11.	12.

1.	2.	3.	4.
5.	6.	7.	8.
9.	10.	11.	12.

1.	2.	3.	4.
5.	6.	7.	8.
9.	10.	11.	12.

1.	2.	3.	4.
5.	6.	7.	8.
9.	10.	11.	12.